Publishing Details

Flipping for Success by Paul Galland, self-published
www.flippingforsuccess.com

@ Paul Galland

First published in 2015 in Australia.

Paperback Version
1st edition 2016

ISBN 978-0-9943658-2-8

Paul is part of a new and emerging type of strategic expert who views the art of strategic management through a wider lens beyond the traditional boundaries of financial and investment capital. Like many others, Paul entered the workforce thinking competition was simply a model based on grow your market as fast as you can and remain competitive on price. Coming from a technology background and witnessing firsthand the various iterations of technology disruptions along the way, he began to see business strategy as something more than a set of operational efficiencies and mergers and acquisitions. This has helped form his underlying philosophy – the art of strategy needs to be reborn and harnessed in a truly innovative, differential way.

Spanning a two-decade IT career, Paul is a senior leader in business-to-technology enterprise planning, challenging the status quo with new and innovative approaches to transforming an organisation. He spent a dozen years serving as an advisory and delivery consultant across nearly every major industry. This breadth of experiences laid the foundation for his book.

Paul has been fortunate enough to work for Deloitte, Sybase and Oracle as well as a host of smaller organisations. He holds a Bachelors and Masters degree from the US, with additional tertiary education in Europe, Latin American and Australia.

This is Paul's first published book.

Table of Contents

Preface

I'm not sure what originally triggered the idea of writing a book on business strategy. I suppose it had crept into my consciousness at some point and then I could not stop thinking about it.

Some three years ago I started to notice a number of conversations with my colleagues about the art of executing business strategy. Many of these conversations were more like rants against why there were many poorly performing business leaders, badly delivered projects, and general frustrations with technology. In each chat, I would find myself making the case for how I truly believed these negative situations could be turned around.

I've suppose I've never shied away from having an opinion. Earlier in my career I usually took an argumentative-styled approach. This often got me into trouble for a number of reasons.

As the years passed, I got older, perhaps a little wiser and those earlier debates gave way to more problem-solving conversations. However, I now find myself going one step beyond those conversations. Lately I am presenting new ideas to business challenges where my audience is receptive and full of enquires, rather than debate.

One by one, those closest to me suggested I should start blogging about the topic. A few even suggested I should write a book. My wife, who had listened to many of these ideas, encouraged me to begin putting pen to paper.

So over the next two years the backbone of this book was formed. Its message has generally remained the same from those earliest of conversations.

I describe the book as part academia, part work experience and part life experience. It attempts to combine my academic, career and personal ramblings, my tapestry of sorts. In another way I suppose this is a snapshot of my life – a work biography. This is my 25-year odyssey with a touch of childhood memories to keep the subject matter real and away from becoming too ivory tower.

When thinking about business strategy here are three questions I have for the reader:

- *How does your organisation invest in its development and execution of strategy?*

- *When was the last time strategy was reviewed to ensure if the desired outcomes were still on target?*

- *What percentage of time does your senior management team spend on the planning side of the business?*

If you're not entirely sure about the answers, then this book is for you. Even if you answered all three, do these answers align to the new business age we have entered?

For many decades businesses weren't required to develop an all-encompassing strategy. The competitive world operated by a set of rules that largely diluted the need to radically transform one's business. The mantra of the day was predominately a simple one; grow the business footprint as quickly as possible and ensure appropriate barriers of trade were in place to keep competitors away.

How times have changed. Some argue, that today we are witnessing the biggest shift in the way business is conducted in some three or four decades! The competitive forces more or less remain the same but the way in which business is conducted has flipped upside down.

No industry is immune either. This business recalibration is a megatrend and is causing a ripple effect that warrants a review of what it means to perform business strategy in today's market. Yesterday's approach to strategic management will not fit tomorrow's.

This is the core principle behind my passion in wanting to write this book. It's to inspire a new generation of business strategists and leaders to take up the call in reshaping how businesses choose to operate and thereby compete. To apply new concepts and ideas which are the fuel behind how an organisation thinks about executing strategy.

Acknowledgements

Like any book, this has been a true labour of love, so a few special mentions are first in order. I would first like to thank Michael E. Porter, whom I quote in this book. Many academics arguably regard him as a living legend of business strategy; I couldn't agree more.

Having earned his PhD in business economics from Harvard, Porter went on to write some 18 books on the topic of competitive strategy. His lateral thinking ability for business strategy is indeed legendary. He famously introduced concepts such as 'value chain' (breaking a business into various components and then analysing each of them) and his 'five forces of competition' into mainstream business thinking.

His concept of 'operational effectiveness' introduced in an essay in 1996 strongly resonated with me. Through my many years of planning, performance and delivery management, I formulated a similar philosophy (at the time having never read any of his work). To me it's a philosophy that is more clearly evident than ever as its being tested right now by a business world experiencing a fundamental and powerful metamorphosis. This book builds upon our mutually shared philosophy by providing additional insights for those board members, leaders and strategy practitioners.

I would also like to thank those professionally closer to me. Hats off to my trusted colleagues who inspired and challenged me to write this book. The numerous thought provoking conversations over the years crystallised many of the concepts contained within. Those I wish to call out who actively assisted in making this book happen are Andy Hurst, Greg Naimo, and Kenny Wong. Those who also provided their support include Rob Livingstone, Jon Tinberg, Muneesh Wadhwa and Catherine Stace. I cannot thank each of you enough.

To my family who has been supportive throughout this process even though they struggled to fully comprehend my role as an enterprise architect. Special thanks to my father and sister Kathryn who performed initial edits to make it more readable.

My acknowledgements would not be complete without a final and most important thank you to my beloved wife who is my rock and closest confidant. She has a passion for how others are treated, and has given me invaluable critique into sections that cover the role of the human condition and change management. I am the luckiest guy alive.

I hope you enjoy the read.

Paul Galland

June 2015

CHAPTER 1:

Introduction

"And it ought to be remembered that there is nothing more difficult to take in hand, more perilous to conduct, or more uncertain in its success, than to take the lead in the introduction of a new order of things."

– Niccolo Machiavelli (1469 – 1527), The Prince, Chapter 4

This quote sums up why I feel so passionate about the future of business and where the art of business strategy fits. This book describes how the successful application of business strategy can be an absolute game changer for an organisation.

Surprisingly, so little strategy is being properly employed today. This is especially true within larger organisations. A McKinsey global survey on corporate strategy conducted in late 2010 reaffirmed just as much. Only one in five executives believed that strategy involved making difficult trade-offs concerning the allocation of their organisation's resources. The report states some other striking statistics:

"In both the boom of the mid-2000s and the financial crisis that followed, many companies did not (or could not) make critical portfolio choices and trade-offs. This may be why so few—just 19

percent of all respondents to this survey—say their companies have a distinct process for developing corporate strategy. Nearly a quarter, however, think their companies should engage in corporate strategy development on an ongoing basis (as opposed to episodically), compared with only 8 percent who say they currently do so" (Birshan, Dye and Hall 2011).

This is some gloomy data. In forming this book I've tried to ensure the content meets two basic objectives. The first is to create broader awareness about how important the practice of strategic management has become in what many describe as a new, consumer-driven age. The second objective is to interlace my own experiences and insights to the use of strategic management practices.

What better way to kick-start this book than to practice what I preach? I'll begin by using what I consider a time-tested and powerful tool that has served me so well in my professional career. It is nothing more than the simple four 'W's (why, what, who, where) as well as the rear guard 'how'. I say the 'rear guard how' as many I engage with will readily jump to the 'how' without processing well enough the other key four Ws.

Nevertheless, I have found 'the how' to be a good conversation starter. These five can regularly to get to the heart of any discussion. So let me take this opportunity to express the nature of this book using these 'five'.

What is this book about?

This book offers a business pitch on how to sell a new strategic approach within your organisation, including how to get your organisation positioned to start doing strategy well. Though it offers a number of tips and approaches to strategy, its purpose is not to be a comprehensive 'how-to' book on performing the art of strategic management.

Instead, it's more like a 'call-to-action' book. A book designed to challenge organisations to adopt better strategic management practices; an impassioned plea for businesses to start taking a closer look at the new role of strategy execution in particular. In the final part of the book I have included some approaches and opportunities businesses can adopt today.

Why write a book on business strategy?

My passion for business strategy runs deep. It has evolved from some startling observations both as a work professional and as a global citizen.

For about the past three decades, our public confidence in business has slowly eroded to a point that there is a crisis of business trust. Many of us now perceive big business as nothing more than corporate greed, driven exclusively by profits above all else.

Past corporate episodes such as the hostile corporate raiding of the 1980s, manufacturing outsourcing of the 1990s, the Dot-Com rise and crash, the sub-prime lending collapse, subsequent Global Financial Crisis and in many countries the great recession, have all produced negative public perceptions about the state of our business world. Whew, just looking at that long list of negative episodes is enough to depress anyone! I sense, like many others, our collective societies are finally on the cusp of something truly different in the way business is conducted this time around.

There is also a changing of the guard in the way technology is consumed. Now consumers drive the investment agenda instead of employers. Many businesses find themselves in unchartered waters. I believe it is one of several catalysts to a new way of conducting business.

Consumers are truly accelerating the pace of change within the business environments we work in, so much so, that business change is now considered constant. This pressure for constant change is fundamentally reshaping the way we think and perform our business planning activities.

However, the path will not be easy and nor will all businesses survive this once-in-two-generation transition. Many organisations continue to be plagued by what I call 'old world management' and process structures. These organisations can no longer cope from the accelerated cycle of change without doing something radically different themselves.

Where there are challenges this big, there are also opportunities waiting. The first businesses to successfully transform themselves gain unique competitive advantages, and the statistics already validate this. As more businesses successfully transform, the public's negative perception of business begins to fade. The new business age promises a workforce who is happier and more engaged at our work places. This may sound like a noble aim, but one that I believe is honestly achievable.

Who should read this book?

Anyone practicing strategy or interested in its discipline would benefit from this book. Board members, C-level, 'heads of' and anyone concerned about their business future should also read this book.

Here's a set of questions for those interested in enhancing strategy for their organisation.

1. *Does your organisation have a central strategy and planning group?*

2. *Has your organisation considered the role of strategy at a higher level than within divisions?*

3. *If your organisation relies upon management consultants to construct, assess or offer options to develop your strategy, then have they been an active part of its execution?*

4. *Does your organisation possess a clear understanding of what innovation or strategy represents to your business?*

5. *Does your executive leadership team or company board actively track the progress of its strategic direction?*

If you answered 'no' or 'not sure' to just *one* of the above questions, then this book can provide value.

Where is strategy most problematic?

From my own time within the workforce, I've come to experience the pain of sudden business disruptions and redirections firsthand. These events unexpectedly send the organisation two steps back before it can actually move forward. I've repeatedly seen investment decisions and leader promises squandered by poor delivery and unrealistic expectations. Sometimes, I must admit, my blood has boiled at the gross miscalculations I've witnessed.

The disconnect between strategic thinking and its execution couldn't be wider. This, I believe, is the most problematic issue in performing strategy today.

I remember a statistic from the mid-1990s that stated more than two-thirds of new investment projects failed to deliver the expected value. Research the field of project delivery today and discover this statistic has remained more or less the same as it did back then.

So why is it that we can't evolve in the planning and delivery of our strategic investments? Are there problems with project execution, project planning, the capital planning governance, or lack of a business vision? Is it something else, or perhaps, all of the above?

Although there have been significant and positive strides within project planning and execution, not enough progress has been made to ensure that planning and delivery outcomes relate back to those strategic management practices. On the contrary, strategic planning has largely been the domain of silo business groups and not a centralised, organisational function.

The reasons for this high rate of failure are indeed diverse, but one underlying truism has continued to bother me for the better part of a decade. Strategic management—or lack thereof—has run counter to the operational pressures and necessities of the business world. That is, until now.

Today's measuring stick for value is quite different from yesteryears. It's designed around business innovation as opposed to specialising in process efficiencies to gain a competitive edge. But shouldn't the approach to business strategy also change to align to these new consumer demands?

There are plenty of strategic management books describing the 'thinking' side of the strategic equation. The science around what constitutes competition is not under scrutiny here. Instead this book will primarily focus on the doing, or execution, side of strategic management.

In a world that has become quite complex and cross-functionally automated, so few have an organisation-wide understanding of this complexity. It's no wonder so few can make sense of it.

To resolve 'the where' problem, I have divided the discussion of strategy into differing views about it. There are of course the traditional fields of marketing and finance to consider but also new views to investigate such as the role of the human condition and the role of technology. Together these views demonstrate a more systemic, multi-disciplinary approach to strategic management.

How is this book organised, and how do I read it?

This book examines disciplines not traditionally associated with business strategy—like the importance of human behaviour, new technology disruptors, change management, social responsibility and the impact of leadership to name a few. Today's strategy requires a broader set of skills to perform strategic management, or the art of strategy. As such, this theme is interwoven into nearly every chapter.

The book is sequenced into three basic parts: A, B and C. In order to understand the context of today's environment, the first part looks at the past. This includes an examination of what strategy is not. Part B examines the role of the human condition and technology as key drivers of strategy. Lastly Part C examines the approaches and challenges in performing strategic management today.

I wrote this book to best be read cover to cover as it lays out a step-by-step process to building the new story of strategy. Nevertheless, many readers have limited time or may have areas of particular interest. For these readers I've segmented the book according to sectional areas of interest.

PART A:

Strategic Management Basics

CHAPTER 2:
Business Strategy, a Brief History

"If you know the enemy and know yourself, you need not fear the result of a hundred battles. If you know yourself but not the enemy, for every victory gained you will also suffer a defeat. If you know neither the enemy nor yourself, you will succumb in every battle."

– Sun Tzu, The Art of War

This quote reflects the importance of strategy in war. The same principle can be applied to business. It's about knowing who you are, your strengths and weaknesses, as well as your competitors, before making choices about the future. Applying Sun Tzu's principle to this book, it's about knowing the context of one's environment before beginning a deeper analysis and investigation.

That is in essence what this chapter is about. Setting the historical scene of business management with a key focus on strategic management. A reflection into understanding what led us to this highly interconnected, yet in some ways dysfunctional, business environment.

About fifty years ago the business world was first introduced to strategic management. It seems like a fitting timeframe to pick up the historical search. To simplify all the complex moving parts, I've divided the various incarnations of business strategic management into three major periods: the dawn of business strategy, the Kaizen game changer, and the Internet game changer.

The dawn of business strategy and boundless opportunities

The practice of strategic management was largely non-existent before the 1960s, so where did it originate? One could make a strong case that the field of strategic management started from the lecture halls within Harvard University.

Throughout the 1950s, a group of professors including George Albert Smith Jr., C. Roland Christensen and, later, Kenneth Andrews, got students contemplating the nature of competition from a strategic context. By the early 1960s, their business policy classes continued to evolve and mature. Kenneth Andrews put several competing elements together as a framework that later became known as the classic SWOT analysis, which stands for strengths, weaknesses, opportunities and threats. This framework was quite popular—as it remains today—and it advanced the young field of strategic management.

By the late 1960s there was plenty of thought leadership circulating along with a known and popular SWOT framework rising in popularity. The field of strategic management was ready to make its appearance into mainstream businesses.

This period has been referred as the 'strategic revolution'. It was a time when people began thinking systemically about a business's approach to growth. The three C's—costs, customers and competitors—emerged during this time. Prior to the revolution, few organisations gave the notion of competition any deep sense of analysis (Emmons 2010).

To illustrate many books concentrated on the internal workings of the company, such as how effective their thought leadership was. None of the books entertained the idea of a company looking over its shoulders to see what its competition was doing (Kiechel 2010).

The revolution meant that business leaders no longer needed to pursue a 'go-it-alone' approach to seeking their company's fortunes. They could, instead, adapt their decision-making to detailed study of their competitive landscape against broader industry trends (Wooldridge 2010). This was considered quite new thinking at the time. It reminds me of just how much we take for granted today.

The four men chiefly behind this revolution were Bruce Henderson, Bill Bain, Fred Gluck and Michael Porter. The first three were chiefs of the three major management consultancy firms: The Boston Consulting Group, Bain & Company and McKinsey & Company. Their collective pioneering work included business strategy models, frameworks and the application of rigorous data analysis.

So much intellectual thinking came out of this period that it guaranteed the firms' prosperity for decades to come. Eventually these firms became synonymous with spearheading business thought leadership for nearly every major global business. They designed frameworks, gathered evidence, and provided insights, which enabled leaders to make meaningful improvements to their organisations.

During this period business boardrooms were experiencing three decades of post-war prosperity and looking for the next big thing. The revolution gave way to boundless engagement opportunities around every corner of the business universe.

As these big-three management consultancy firms grew their client base, their models become ever more sophisticated. In turn, this sophistication became ever more analytical as time passed. By the 1970s, the revolution had become largely institutionalised. A business leader would be a fool for not seeking counsel about their future growth plans.

It is here where I make a special mention to a gentleman named Taylor. Frederick Taylor (1856-1915) is considered by many as the founder of the theory of scientific management, a theory based largely on numbers to derive efficiencies.

Though he did not live to see the theory's crossover application to business, by the 1920s many were applying his theory to how goods are produced and distributed on a mass scale. The theory concentrated on finding the application of scientific methods within industrial production. Perhaps most famous was Henry Ford's 'mass production' line concept, which had its origin in Taylor thinking (Kaston et al. 1995).

Eventually Taylor's ideas started to be applied beyond the factory floor, finding its influence into the white-collar world of management. By the 1960s, when the strategy revolution was well and truly underway, Taylorism was being applied as a philosophy to discovering competitive differentiation.

This version of Taylorism helped shape the American business engine toward ever-greater management efficiency. Walter Keichel, a strategic management historian, coins this new version of Taylorism as 'Greater Taylorism'. It is described as "the corporation's application of sharp-pencilled analytics, this time not to the performance of an individual worker (how fast a person could load bars of pig iron or reset a machine), but more widely to the totality of its functions and processes (Kiechel 2010)."

Number crunching was everywhere and the business world smiled. But just when everything looked so rosy for the growing field of strategic management, two un-related forces appeared and upset the prevailing thinking. Yet they each had something in common, the value of people.

First, by the early 1980s, the success of strategic management began to bring about scrutiny and self-examination. In 1982, a popular book was released called *In Search of Excellence*, which argued that the obsession with strategy was ignoring the human equation within organisations. The second force was the economic powerhouse of the Japanese economy that began to take the world by storm. In doing so it introduced its own unique variables into the strategic equation, shaking up the global business world in the process.

The kaizen game changer

If we had a time machine that could transport us back in time to America during the early 1980s, we would see business panic everywhere. This panic was not American in origin, but Japanese. America had just come out of a minor recession, a confidence drainer in its own right. Pick up any business periodical of the day and you would read how the Japanese were world leaders —able to run a business better, more efficiently and with better quality than most U.S. counterparts.

Many a CEO in the U.S. stood in awe and watched this Asian juggernaut begin to saturate the U.S. with its own goods. I might have been young, but I clearly remember 'Made in Japan' tags everywhere. I remember reading stories about how the Japanese acquired the famous Rockefeller Center in New York. Some even suggested that after the Rockefeller acquisition, the Japanese were looking to purchase the Statue of Liberty. Hollywood even got into the act by releasing a number of films, like 'Gung Ho' that starred Tom Hanks, dedicated to this Japanese business tidal wave.

So what went wrong with the new strategic revolution? Wasn't this revolution supposed to spur a new age of business dominance for the U.S.? To seek answers, we need to turn to an Asian philosophy that underpinned this business tidal wave.

The philosophy was based on the concept of 'Kaizen'. Though the Western world has struggled to effectively translate this word, it's commonly translated as 'change, good', or 'change for the better'. In fact, the concept of Kaizen is actually quite old and found referenced in Chinese hanzi, Korean hanja and Japanese kanji (Traveler 2009).

In western business literature Kaizen is a widely seen as a philosophy focusing on process continuous improvement, traditionally associated with the engineering and manufacturing industries. Studying the philosophical origins of Kaizen a bit deeper reveals it differs quite markedly from Taylorism.

Kaizen is to take it apart and put back together in a better way. What is taken apart is usually a process, system, product, or service. Kaizen is a daily activity whose purpose goes beyond improvement. It is also a process that, when done correctly, humanizes the workplace, eliminates hard work (both mental and physical), and teaches people how to do rapid experiments using the scientific method and how to learn to see and eliminate waste in business processes (Owl 2007).

Whilst Taylorism was strictly about the application of scientific management, the value of the worker was left out in the cold. Kaizen goes beyond Taylorism to incorporate the value of the worker to the process. In Kaizen philosophy everyone participates, from the CEO to the floor operator. It requires long-term discipline to make it work. Kaizen has been successfully incorporated into Japanese management concepts such as Toyota's Total Quality Management and labour relations.

Speaking of Total Quality Management, Toyota's rise to become one of the biggest companies in the world was not accidental. Their management team's visit to Detroit in the 1950s is now legendary. Instead of being impressed with the auto plants they visited, they were most drawn to a visit at a nearby American supermarket and how it kept track of all its stock. At the end of each day the supermarket reordered what it had sold during the day.

From a retail perspective we now take this for granted but at the time the concept was quite innovative to the visiting Japanese delegation. They saw an opportunity to provide qualitative improvements to their existing stock controls. Upon returning to Japan they convinced their management to replicate it, and the approach got the tick of approval.

Toyota's production system is based in large part on Kaizen. It considers itself to be a learning organisation, constantly reflecting and evolving. The worker's input is just as important to the knowledge of the company as the company knowledge and the improvements made.

This was the missing link for U.S.-based companies that looked at process efficiencies solely as a numbers game. It wasn't long before western companies started to embrace Kaizen philosophy by placing equal importance on the value of worker talent.

Perhaps the best example of blending Kaizen principles to western business practices was General Electric under the leadership of Jack Welsh. His famous Work-Out program not only reinvented GE to become a powerhouse global giant, it was emulated throughout the American business landscape. MBA programs subsequently sought to reference it, as did mine some ten years ago.

The GE program was created with the objective to eliminate management fat and decision-making inefficiencies. As its footprint and success within GE grew, its role expanded. The Work-Out program was always bound to three key principles:

- *All Work-Out sessions involved 45 to 100 people in cross-functional and cross-level groups, to provide the kind of combustive diversity not seen from intact teams.*

- *All sessions led by a senior executive leader, who could not just give his or her blessing but was required to take part wholeheartedly.*

- *Lastly and most controversially, the leader had to say "yes" or "no" on the spot to every idea presented at the session. Taking an idea under advisement for study was not an option (Kleiner 2003).*

Both the Toyota and GE examples provided their employees with an engaging platform on which to voice their ideas. GE's Work-Out sessions created an even playing field for discussions between staff and management. The management hierarchy could not impede on the merits of having an open forum. The open forum style was able to cut across management lines, seeking to improve cross-functional GE business activities. Even after Jack Welsh retired in 2002, GE management teams continued to use this program.

It's worth remembering this was still a time when being leaner and more efficient was *the* competitive differentiation. Size also mattered as it was seen as a competitive advantage. Smaller businesses had to navigate the 'tyranny of distance' to stay competitive. Today this is no longer true with the arrival of mass communication and online commerce.

The Kaizen period also marked the explosion of company access to new, favourable global markets. The signing of numerous free trade agreements between countries was a significant contributor to this access. This meant larger companies could capitalise on these new foreign opportunities faster. They held a comparable advantage over smaller competitors who needed more capital and internal capabilities to make the international leap – that tyranny of distance again.

Though some smaller companies did manage to organically grow into these new markets, the best way to seize opportunity was through the popular method of the day, mergers and acquisitions, or M&A. For me the popular 1980s movie 'Wall Street' remains one of those memorable movies that capture's the euphoria of this period.

The lean, recession-led 80s quickly gave way to the greedy 80s. M&A activity started to dominate Wall Street and other global trading houses. New capital flooded into the markets. By the late 80s it truly became a period of great global expansion for the largest of businesses. Investor cash infusion and hefty returns on profits continued to justify their expansionist ways.

The tyranny of distance was indeed a beast of a problem for smaller companies. Another way to illustrate this distance problem is to borrow the entrepreneurial concept of blue and red oceans. The newly emerging markets overseas were at first considered 'blue ocean' opportunities for the larger, western businesses. These companies quickly moved into these new markets by using their established brands and marketing power to gain a favourable business position.

Local businesses were quickly swept away. They were simply outmatched to compete in terms of volume and price. It was especially true if a free-trade agreement was put in place. Government protectionist policies, the one thing local competitors could use as a safety net, were largely inadequate, absent or removed when an agreement was signed. There were of course local business exceptions but the growth numbers of large global corporations during this period are testament to some of the unbalanced competitive forces that were at play.

This 'blue ocean' existed as long as there were one, or maybe two, global competitors feasting in this undiscovered ocean (read market). However, the ocean started turning red as more sharks (numerous other western competitors) began to ply the waters.

The classic example is McDonalds. The company was the first fast food chain to establish itself in many new markets overseas, but was later followed by Burger King, Pizza Hut and Kentucky Fried Chicken.

Noticing its own growth opportunities overseas, a yet bigger shark entered the picture when PepsiCo bought a string of fast food companies in the early 90s and further expanded their global footprint. In 1997 they spun off many of these same businesses to create Tricon Global Restaurants. The spin off allowed PepsiCo to generate additional cash to go on yet another series of company acquisitions. Meanwhile the new business entity Tricon rebranded itself 'Yum! Brands' and continued to expand their own global footprint by opening up additional fast food stores overseas.

With brand power established the ocean becomes increasingly redder. The quality of goods starts to diminish as the global fight intensifies on price and volume. The process efficient business world continues to use ever more fanciful instruments to stay ahead its competitors.

Examples of these instruments included outsourced labour agreements as a form of cheaper labour tactics, and the increasing importance of patents used to tighten market barriers. Behind it all was an increasing attention to legal affairs, company rights and entitlements. The number of lawyers entering the profession significantly shot up in the United States. Corporate civil cases exploded, as did payouts and settlements.

Companies also employed their own barriers of entry to fiercely protect their hard won markets. Some of these market barriers were in the form of non-compete agreements, and aggressive legal pursuits to protect patents. Still others managed to persuade foreign governments to pass local legislation that gave them an unfair trade advantage over their competition.

In order to stay competitive global companies also turned to technology automation as another form of cheaper labour tactics. The pursuit of greater efficiency led to more complex operating environments. This in turn drove up the need for greater forms of specialisation, which in itself became a new buzzword.

The role of 'specialist' and the concept of 'specialisation' helped to address the complex and ever-increasing demands of process efficiencies. Some of these specialists ran critical IT systems, or knew how to number crunch, or were gifted at contract negotiations or could manage high-profile projects. All these skill sets could be found within every large organisation.

These were the individuals that mattered most to the organisation. Specialists by nature are always in high demand so keeping them requires more attention focused on their wants and needs. Company travel perks and stock options were tools of trade to try and retain many of these white-collar specialists.

As operational efficiencies matured, technology matured alongside it. Technology may have replaced paper-based systems, but that doesn't mean the paper trail was eliminated. In many cases the paper trail simply went digital.

Eventually technology became embedded into the complete value chain. A classic example is discrete manufacturing, an industry that produces products like automobiles, computers and appliances. This industry relies on tight inventory and production line controls to maximise its unit outputs. By the late 1990s, technology-based business systems were monitoring, regulating and optimising the efficiency of goods produced in manufacturing.

My first taste of this powerful use of technology was in 1996 while working as a technical consultant. I was assigned to a large process efficiency program at one of the world's largest rubber manufacturers. At the time, the company was a billion-dollar business producing much of the world's rubber belts and hoses.

The program's objective was to install and configure a fully integrated set of technologies to help run its warehouse, inventory and production line business systems. Once finished, the program was estimated to save the company $1m a day in automation efficiencies (so I was told). With numbers like that, the program had the full attention of its executives and board. They saw it as something that would save their company from extinction.

Their other competitors were also doing the same thing, as was many of their suppliers. The message was simple: integrating technology into their business processes was a requirement to stay competitive.

Process automation may increase efficiency but it can cause significant losses from unexpected events because there is very little slack in the system. It can take longer to bring a manufacturing process fully back to operational status from an unplanned event if it is not properly designed well.

A good example is the massive 2011 earthquake that rattled much of the eastern side of Japan. The earthquake knocked out production plants for many of Japan's automotive heavyweights. The car industry took 6-12 months to recover even though each of these manufacturers was globally based and all used the most advanced technologies. The excerpt below epitomised the technological dependencies within the industry:

> *A leading analyst is warning that the Australian car industry will be under threat if production in Japan does not resume soon. The economic fallout from Japan's twin disasters has some of nation's signature industries suspend production. Electronics manufacturer Sony has limited production running at 15 of its 25 Japanese plants, and car makers Toyota, Honda and Mitsubishi, have all wound back operations. For the most part, it was not direct damage that forced the closure of car plants across Japan. Instead, a shortage of supplies, including electricity, has made the resumption of manufacturing difficult (Hall 2011).*

For those companies who were first to market with cutting-edge technology automation, they possessed a competitive advantage – the potential to growing faster. I use the word 'potential' because implementing a new system that reduces inefficiencies doesn't necessarily lead to higher sales growth. It simply reduces costs, generating savings that can be applied for growth initiatives elsewhere.

From a competitive viewpoint, the technology investment is only short lived. As more competitors upgrade and automate their own business systems, that competitive edge shrinks as the necessity to sink capital into it increases.

In an essay entitled 'What is Strategy?', Michael Porter writes "few companies have competed successfully on the basis of operational effectiveness over an extended period, and staying ahead of rivals gets harder every day. Competitors can quickly imitate management techniques, new technologies, input improvements, and superior ways of meeting customers needs (Porter, Kim and Mauborgne 2011, 6)."

Much like labour off shoring, now considered quite a mature business practice, earlier technology investments meant operational efficiencies were *not* a game changer for many businesses. Yes, there were clear exceptions, but for the vast majority of cases, technology was a must-have investment to stay with the competition.

The name of the competitive game was to be the first to arrive, and use the organisation's size and brand to stay ahead. Once ahead, maintain that position by creating more efficiencies to ensure the business continued to compete on price and volume. Protect that lead by building a legal circle around intellectual property and new contractual arrangements.

If a company could stick to this plan it would see increasing profits, keeping its shareholders happy whilst exploring opportunities to acquire more of its competitors. With business principles of globalisation and free trade as mandates for growth and the tyranny of distance the single most competitive rule of the road, large companies held court over others.

The notion of greed through ever bigger profits precipitated western culture. Western consumers largely turned a blind eye to this, giving the nod of approval by drinking from the 'age of materialism' cup. And so the cycle went.

From a business strategy context, global expansion into less mature markets created new opportunities for strategic research around acquisitions. Management consultancy firms were again well placed to assist in these M&A transactions.

These firms had at their disposal a diverse team of specialist strategists to help detail an M&A transaction. By the late 1990s, at the height of the dot-com bubble, it was difficult to find a staff-level business strategist who reported to the CEO or had an influential role amongst the C-level stakeholders. These roles were absent from the top echelon of executive teams.

It all reached a low point when strategic talk around the leadership table came with the notion that strategy was something that others knew better about than their own people. Would the executive board call in the strategy experts who better knew what the competition was doing to point them in the right direction?

Describing the competitive landscape was akin to herding cattle to ever-shorter destinations. Had the operational efficiency business world truly run its course?

The high number of failed acquisitions suggested so. Much of that earlier research was divorced from the operational side of the business. The research either did not properly consider the people side of the equation, or grossly underestimated the effort to integrate disparate process automated systems.

However, it wasn't the strategic thinkers that ushered in a new way of approaching business competition. The dawn of a new business paradigm came from a fundamentally different area of society. The new approach ushered in a business climate where leaders began to better address organisational change, both systemically and at a cultural level.

It changed the competitive landscape once again; the 'war on talent' had begun. The priority was no longer on opening up new markets. The business landscape was transitioning from a 'people matter' Kaizen view to something akin to 'people make the difference'.

What was the source to this new business period? Funny enough it had to do with how people started to communicate in ways no one ever envisioned.

The Internet game changer

I must be getting older. I now hear people talk about the idea of globalisation and the Internet as almost one in the same thing. I suppose the details of history lose focus as time marches forward.

I'd like to take a quick trip down memory lane. The term 'globalisation' and its cousin, 'free trade', have been around longer than the Internet and were first coined in the greedy 80s. The two terms gained more media attention well into the early 90s. Research any newspaper or magazine from that period and the odds are good these terms pop up quite easily.

In 1991 Tim Berners-Lee released the 'WorldWideWeb' to the public domain. Just two years later, the widely popular Mosaic browser allowed the Internet to go mainstream in a big way.

I remember this period well. I guess I could say my long technology career started by being asked to build a website for a non-profit organisation I worked for at the time. I built the whole website using the simplest of tools, Microsoft's Notepad utility. This was 1994 and I remember we had the site up and running an entire year before McDonald's had theirs. By 1995, Internet hype was everywhere in the media.

The following year I went to work for Oracle. Shortly after joining, the company famously stated that it was moving its entire $1b+ business onto the Internet. At the time it was a bold statement. To Oracle's credit, within a few years the company did in fact re-engineer their entire product line to run from the Internet. That said other decisions were not as successful, such as the mid-1990s attempt to launch the 'network computer'. Nevertheless, for IT companies it was a period of great promise and opportunities.

As explored in the prior section, the business landscape was full of fierce competition where the main game was all about size and first to new markets. Globalisation and free trade were the primary channels for growth and expansion.

One of the first kinks in this way of doing business appeared by how information could be exposed and disseminated through the Internet. I can clearly remember that penned phrase, 'a new information age', from the late 1990s. It stoked and fuelled many stock markets around the world. Greater information dissemination alone did not and could not upset the traditional business order, but it was a significant building block to something quite different.

In just the span of half a decade the Internet had grown from a simple information channel to an ecommerce platform for small businesses. These businesses played by a new rulebook, which ignored that 'tyranny of distance' problem. Smaller businesses could instantly offer a global audience their goods and services without having to physically set up a storefront. They could skirt around and potentially leapfrog their larger competitors who many weren't paying attention to this new revenue channel.

The wave of new Internet technologies fuelled new and better business processes. These processes enabled businesses to cheaply target new markets, reduce the price of market entry, and; thereby, reduce their marketing and public relations costs. These same processes also helped cut transportation time and costs to almost nil, especially where products and services were fully digitised.

A typical example from this period was the generation of an electronic invoice. The traditional way of performing a transaction was to print an invoice, place it in an envelope, drop it into the mail and then await payment from the customer *before* sending their goods.

The debut and subsequent proliferation of Acrobat Reader meant an electronic invoice could be easily produced in a 'PDF' format. A clever series of Java-based instructions allowed the transaction to be completed electronically using a person's email box rather than dropping it into a postal box. The entire process was near instantaneous and the technology relatively cheap to deploy.

Small businesses no longer needed to heavily invest in this important business function, nor did they have to wait for payment to arrive via snail mail. Their goods could arrive quicker than larger companies took to send out their goods. As many often say, the Internet truly levelled the business playing field.

Perhaps even more important, consumers could now access data easier and faster than ever before. The Internet had become loaded with millions of web pages exposing data about many things. But was the data delivering true information to consumers? And why does this matter?

Data alone does not mean anything. I always chuckle when I think about data because I was a big fan of the hit TV show 'Cheers', especially the character Cliff Clavin. He was the famous postman who sat next to Norm. He would always share some useless fact that really never meant anything.

Information, on the other hand, is data about data. It is metadata, or data that has been interpreted to give some contextual meaning and purpose. Information allows us to make intelligent decisions in our lives. Data is harnessed so that information can be gleaned for our purposes.

I tend to think of the Internet's information highway built in two stages. At first the Internet was spewing out reams of published data to the mass public. In the first years of the Internet how much of this data was really harnessed to provide real value? Publishing content may have been interesting to read but beyond that, not much value.

The Internet was more of a cool thing to look at than to leverage for our own purposes. Perhaps the lone exceptions were news stories, scientific studies and product marketing material. Some of us may have found value in our lives by reading this stuff.

However, these examples demonstrate content that was already available in other mediums. Web site administrations simply copied and pasted this content onto the Internet. The WorldWideWeb was hardly the type of place that would change our lives.

The second stage of the information highway debuted when the Internet became a more active community platform. It offered such things as ecommerce transactions and the ability to participate in online discussions about hot issues of the day. The dawn of the blogger had arrived.

People could participate on the web by making purchases for things they liked, as well as contributing to what others had to say about a given topic. Eventually banking and government services came to the Internet, and finally the arrival and explosive growth of social media.

As the Internet continues to mature, so too does the maturity of online information. People are no longer just reading items of interest. They are using it as a social and community extension to their everyday lives. For many of us the information we access today profoundly affects our consumer choices and life decisions we intend to make.

Twenty years on we are using the Internet in ways once thought un-imaginable. Today we place more trust in trip advisor feedback than a brochure about a travel package. We only look for 4 or 5 review stars, no matter what type of service we are shopping for. Many of us investigate a future employer by reading anonymous and honest commentary from employees who work or have worked there. We are tweeting and making new social connections by participating in what's trending. The list goes on.

The Internet is not just affecting our individual lives. Social media platforms also harness and spawn greater community and social awareness.

Special interest communities use the power of social media as another form of street protest. Protests can be mobilised quicker and on larger scales, the Internet knows no geographic boundaries. The Arab Spring, which started in Tunisia and quickly spread to neighbouring Egypt, was in large part inspired by disenfranchised youth not being able to protest in the streets. They took to using a powerful tool they had at their fingertips.

Subtler community-inspired activism is also well and truly alive. These like-minded social groups are generating positive results against global companies who are perceived to be insensitive to the communities they affect. Examples are plenty such as off-shored child labour, the continued release of harmful bi-products, or unsafe work practices.

Richard Branson in his book, 'Screw Business As Usual', writes about this social awareness force. "Companies are springing up that use the Internet and social media to build powerful communities that are radically reinventing how we live in the world (Branson 2013, 319)." He later argues there is a pressing need for businesses to once again take up the 'corporate social responsibility' (or CSR) mantel.

CSR was a business initiative that first appeared in the 1980s and ran throughout the 1990s before succumbing as a business priority. The lack of CSR business sustainability was in part because businesses saw it as a value-add, a feel-good story to help positively sell the brand. This reason no longer applies today. In many western countries, the citizenry now *expect* that their own global companies run respectable and socially conscious set of global operations.

The practice of globalisation and free trade may have started out as business principles based on 'first-to-market' and do all that is necessary, no matter the societal costs, to stay #1. However these two terms have evolved into something today that appears a bit softer and gentler.

In today's interconnected global village, globalisation and free trade may even translate into a kind of 'do unto others as you would do unto yourself' motto. Those businesses that continue to operate their overseas branches from yesterday's world run the risk of severely damaging their brand as well as support from their local communities.

It's not just unfair work practices that are in the social magnifying glass. Environmental awareness has once again climbed the social awareness ladder. It is now arguably as important as it was during the 1960s and 70s.

Some of today's environmental issues remain a holdover. Whale hunting and energy consumption immediately come to mind. Many others are new like climate change, genetic food modification, poor animal husbandry or inhumane livestock slaughtering practices.

Perhaps the most important difference from the 20th century movement and today is a new target audience. In the 1960s and 70s national and state governments were on the firing line to do something about environmental issues. Today, consumers are now targeting businesses, as well as continue to press politicians.

The Internet becoming a significant medium for consumer activism and competitive advantage has also ushered in the importance technology has on business strategy. As technology investments have moved out of the corporate back-office (the Kaizen period) and into the hands of the consumers, the importance of technology as a key strategic driver has steadily increased.

No longer does a business force the introduction of technologies to their customers. It is now becoming the reverse. Customers are demanding a mobility service that offers x, or a product that does y. If a business cannot deliver that capability, the consumer will leave and find it elsewhere.

This reversal is affecting not only corporate IT departments, but non-IT business units as well. They are all on the receiving end of these customer demands. As I'll explore later in the book, this subtle shift in technology ownership from business to consumer is having a huge cultural effect on the internal workings of an organisation.

Caring for the planet, conducting business in a more ethical manner and better listening to customer concerns are all new conditions for businesses to carefully consider. Whether intended or not, the dawn of the Internet has substantially changed the competitive landscape of businesses. It might have taken several decades for the Internet to become the primary medium of such forces, but the mass communication foundation had indeed been laid.

Business strategy now requires a rethink

I've read some academics are heralding a new, third industrial revolution. This third revolution has its foundations around the Internet, renewable energies and environmental sustainability. It's markedly different from the second wave of the early 20th century. That wave witnessed innovations around the gasoline-powered automobile, electricity, refrigeration, and radio/TV to name a few.

What struck me by this observation is how many of those earlier innovations are still with us today, innovations that first developed a century ago. Don't get me wrong. A car today is not the same as one from Henry Ford's day, but the basic elements and principles behind gasoline-powered cars remain.

Instead of evolving to a transportation vehicle quite radically different (like a flying scooter), we have chosen to stay with our beloved cars. Up to about the start of the millennium the same held true for many other earlier innovations. Over the past century we continually tweaked them, always seeking to improve upon the same basic designs.

Yet in the past decade or so, there has been a flurry of radically new designs not seen in frequency and number since the last revolutionary period. Don't believe me? Take a moment to think about the advances just in medicine and robotics to see what is just around the corner.

This view of a third industrial revolution aligns well with why organisations prioritised and performed operational efficiencies for the past three or four decades. The widgets and gadgets produced by these businesses (bar a few exceptions) where designs borrowed from an earlier time. There was little in the way of new innovations to disrupt business competition. The competitive model never really changed from its original design. It was always about tweaking a process here, or opening up a new market there by copying from an existing one elsewhere.

Yes in western economies, life has indeed become better for many of us. However, it wasn't through a wave of new innovations as much as it was from lowering the price on goods to make them affordable for anyone to buy. Many of these goods did indeed have improvements to their original designs. They were positioned and sold as new features to make it appear we were buying some new innovative product.

As examined earlier, eventually the competitive model based on operational efficiencies started to fizzle. There were no more untapped markets in abundance. With many competitive waters red with sharks and with the inherit value of designs becoming more antiquated and outdated, the world became ripe for new innovative ideas in the way we behave and make choices.

This particular wave, like the prior two before it, is built upon unique business and technology innovations allowing society to *leap* forward, instead of simply moving forward. Any wave by nature is quite disruptive. It eliminates businesses that choose to ignore these societal forces.

It's time for a quick quiz. Think of industries that have been globally disrupted in just the past five years. Ok, please pause from reading for just a moment... Got a few? How many could you name?

My choices of notable industries that have experienced severe disruption include: media, music, higher education, healthcare, Not-For-Profits, telecommunications, retail, energy, banking, and technology. That's ten major industries I could name within half a minute! I cannot think of a time in my own lifetime where this much disruption is occurring across a wide set of industries.

These disruptions are causing a major recalibration to traditional industry models. Some of these industries are still undergoing a transformation whilst others are coming to the end of theirs. These disruptions do vary per country. Some disruptions tend to ripple across the globe whilst others are near instantaneous.

And there are industries right now on the cusp of joining my list. The consulting industry appears to be one of those positioned for a major recalibration. In fact, I honestly believe nearly every industry will ultimately be affected in the next five to ten years. We are living in unsettling business times.

With so much business disruption happening from a range of diverse forces business strategy requires a serious rethink to better help organisations make sense of the madness. I quote a well-travelled expert on business innovation.

An era in which fanatical cost-cutting, downsizing, lean Six-Sigma, mergers and acquisitions, supply chain management, off shoring or outsourcing are no longer the basis for competitive advantage. These practices may undoubtedly have created some value in the old days, for example when Jack Welch was running GE, but business leaders on the whole are recognizing that times have changed. Jeff Immelt, GE's current CEO, says, "The only answer for us today is innovation." And Ginni Rometty, President and CEO of IBM, echoed these words when she stated that, "For CEOs today, it's all about achieving growth through innovation (Gibson 2013)."

It warms my heart to see organisations investing in strategy to provide some insights and answers to this new innovative world. Questions abound such as:

- *How do organisations prepare themselves?*

- *How do they retrain their management to ensure their customers come first?*

- *Should strategy be a centralised or decentralised function, and does it matter?*

- *Should strategy be defined differently in this new business landscape, or is it the same with a different approach applied?*

- *What type of skills might a business strategist possess?*

- *Should the business strategist continue to be outsourced to management consultant firms, or should strategic management be incubated internally within the organisation?*

CHAPTER 3:
What are the Strategic Boundaries

"The aim of argument, or of discussion, should not be victory, but progress."

– Joseph Joubert (1754-1824), French moralist

The major problem with strategy is trying to fully appreciate what it is. Everyone claims to do it and definitions are aplenty. A random LinkedIn profile search these days will easily reveal nearly everyone has expertise in it. It's as if everyone needs the word 'strategy' on their resume to be perceived as effective managers and leaders.

Many books, blogs and essays attempt to define the meaning of strategy, the art of managing strategy, or strategic management. Strategy will always be a broad topic of discussion, and it will remain a hard thing to define exactly.

In fact, many find the term so confusing they have given up on using it for fear of causing confusion to others. Adrian Woolridge writing for the Wall Street Journal described strategy in the business world as 'somewhat confused' (Wooldridge 2010). For a number of colleagues I have worked with, it evoked a strong and negative reaction that alerted me to tread carefully around the topic. Therefore, trying to define it during a period of significant business re-orientation would only complicate matters.

So maybe I can do something different and discuss what strategy *isn't*. My aim is to identify some loose boundaries around strategy by calling out what it isn't. It's to close the gaps in communication that exists when conversations inevitably turn to the theme of strategy.

In defining what it is not, I believe it's possible to eliminate the most unflattering misconceptions of strategy that delivers little to no value. By identifying and staying clear of these falsehoods, we move closer to the essence of how strategy provides solid business value. My approach is to present three simple rules of what strategy isn't and then summarise what remains.

Rule #1: Strategy does not exist without an achievable vision

At its core, strategy cannot be initiated without first having a pre-conceived 'imagine if' scenario. It's a picture of an ideal state not yet achieved, and is the anchor of strategy. Without a vision, investing in the long-term viability of the business simply should not proceed.

A vision can be thought much like the old adage, 'If you don't know where you're going, you'll never get there'. Strategy cannot exist without an achievable vision. Without a vision, it becomes an impossible thing to do. So there it is, the first indication of what strategy isn't.

This rule may sound obvious but digging a bit deeper the rule also eliminates tactical business tweaks that will continually occur. I like to call these 'tweaks' operational efficiencies. Strategy will always be implemented through a series of tactics, but here I refer to *operational* priorities as opposed to visionary priorities. In every business operational priorities are a necessity because nothing truly stays unchanging within a business's operating climate.

41

However, if there are too many of these operational tweaks performed without an alignment to a vision or direction, then these can lead to an inefficient delivery of capital. There's also a tendency to focus on these efficiencies because they are tactical and live in the present, as opposed to more strategic, or long-tail, growth priorities. The risks of doing nothing, or simply continuing to tweak the operations of the business without knowing a direction, are usually the highest risk to the organisation.

Once a vision is articulated and endorsed, a business target-state can then be constructed. This is a more detailed dissection of the vision. It is an excellent tool to form a baseline for the strategic execution plan, and also serves as an excellent communication tool to a wider business audience. From a well-crafted business target-state, the vision now has a sense of purpose and direction.

The challenge is usually not in creating a vision and corresponding target state. These items are generally considered the easier part. Instead, the challenge is crafting a solid and effective strategic execution plan, or SEP for short.

Some may call an SEP a business plan. Similar to the word strategy, there's much confusion about what an effective business plan is. Adding to the confusion is a plethora of business plan templates available. The variance of these is remarkable.

From my work experience I have seen a number of business plans that appear more like delivery guides for attaining better operational efficiencies. It is rare I come across a business plan that traces the business aims and corresponding tasks back to the strategic vision and business target-state. The difficulty in choosing the right planning template is symptomatic of the next rule.

Rule #2: The art of strategy is not a fragmented exercise

Once again this rule seems obvious. However as described in the previous rule, operational efficiencies continue to be treated of higher business priority than the desire to take the harder, visionary road.

The past three decades saw worker specialisation reign supreme. Planning initiatives at the C-level were generally reserved for an M&A deal, or to trumpet a new slogan around achieving higher growth. This is hardly the stuff of innovative, independent thinking.

When a business decides to hold an off-site strategy session, there's a tendency to bring in industry specialists. The specialists describe what the competition is doing. Strategic thinking can be simply about how to stay a nose ahead of the competition to position the business for continued growth.

This form of strategic planning I refer to as 'application of process efficient' (APE). It revolves around fixing duplicate business functions and processes to achieve greater savings and efficiencies (in staying one step ahead of the competition).

An organisation's leadership may have stated a bold version, for example to open a new market. The APE view however muddies the waters by ensuring priority is given to efficiency versus the strategic imperative itself. This APE view remains a carry-over from the Kaizen world of competition and unfortunately, this view very much remains a powerful force.

Let me illustrate a typical capital planning process (CPP) to demonstrate how the APE can negate strategic progress. Most CPPs are usually held once a year in line with budgetary planning. The aim is to better guide the organisation about how and where it spends new monies.

The approach to how this is done usually allows an opportunity for negotiation and compromise between the differing business units. They debate the rationale over how to prioritise the capital expenditure. Back room influencing and deal-making may even occur.

During the CPP each business unit finds itself in a difficult position. Each not only must consider what the new company vision means to them, but also consider operational process tweaks they will be also measured on. If the KPIs of a business unit have not been properly adjusted to the strategic execution plan, as most are not, the business unit 'head of' will likely choose their own KPI as a priority. In some organisations the CPP is completely hijacked by APE-like behaviour and outcomes.

This scenario paints a typical business silo environment where each business unit makes decisions largely independent of the greater organisational good. The larger the company size, more likely there is a higher number of silos.

Business silos add increased complexity within the governance process. The result is increased planning complexity, which generally waters down the value of strategy against the need to meet operational efficiencies. Left unchecked, these APE-influenced planning cycles have an unintended and adverse effect on organisation-wide transformation initiatives.

Have you personally worked for a medium to large organisation and can recall a story about how the left hand of the business did not understand or communicate with the right hand? In my own experience as a delivery consultant for a dozen years, I probably worked with some fifty organisations. I can recall countless examples of this—too many to name.

How can a company-wide strategic plan be executed well if many business units never speak to one another? This brings me to rule number two: the art of strategy is not a fragmented exercise. A strategic plan at some stage needs a well thought out execution path. Without one, fragmented activities and lack of cohesion will erode the leader's vision.

Ideally the execution plan should include senior management input. After all they are the boots on the ground to deliver the vision.

Too often leaders choose to put their faith into a select few to come up with the execution.

It's right to believe strategy is about making tough choices and forcing people to move outside of their comfort zone. However, the creation of the execution plan needs to be inclusive, not secretive in nature. Without full buy-in from senior management, the strategy is doomed from the start.

Strategy as a practice cannot be seen as a siloed business exercise, planned and executed in isolation from the rest of the organisation. Michael Porter sums it up best in an essay he wrote stating, "Strategy is creating fit among a company's activities. The success of a strategy depends on doing many things well—not just a few—and integrating among them (Porter, Kim and Mauborgne 2011, 28)." Ahem Michael.

Rule #3: Strategy is not a one-off process done every 3 or 5 years

Does your organisation employ some smart-minded consultants every few years to develop your strategy? Only to find that when their engagement ends, so ends the execution of that strategy?

If strategy is simply a business activity just to tick some management boxes every so often, then is the organisation really serious about how it attempts to transform itself? Can it actually commit to following a long-term transformation journey?

Many times those that don't fully commit to their strategy are perceived as having one foot in and one foot out. These types of stakeholders clearly appreciate the need to do something but would rather test the water first to see how deep it is. This hesitancy can be quite dangerous within an organisation. Employees interpret their leadership as being noncommittal, unsure or confused as to what to do.

Not fully investing in a strategy can also be systematic to an 'ivory tower' situation. An ivory tower is where a few top brass, plus a consultant or two, would sit in a room to whiteboard their new strategy in isolation from the organisation.

They may shop it around the organisation for staff buy-in, but the activity is perceived as a top-down approach that stays, well up in the tower. It's easy to think of the ivory tower as just another business silo. Those who live in it often pontificate to annoy the many. There is no buy-in at the operational level.

Think of the times you have been in a staff meeting on the day of a new strategic announcement. How many did you spot cringing and gritting their teeth in anticipation? Not only is the new strategy largely a surprise to them, the perception is reinforced that the top brass think they know best and are telling the organisation where it should go and how hard the road will be.

We all know what happens next. Following the announcement, a number of back-room discussions occur amongst the troops on the ground. However unlike military personnel who have been trained for an upcoming battle, these troops have not been properly trained in the finer art of change management.

The conversations therefore are largely negative, and in some cases spiteful against management, who 'don't know what they are talking about'. Letting this typical scenario run its natural course, the organisation determines the adoption of their strategy will require a substantial amount of capital to prepare their staff for a business transformation.

It didn't have to be this way. Top brass have dropped the ball and are now trying to force a change on their staff with no buy-in. Legions of specialised consultants then descend upon the organisation to prepare it for this arduous journey of transformational change.

Does it always have to be this hard? This ivory tower scenario has traditionally been perceived as an adversarial corporate exercise with little in the way of inclusivity and transparency.

Strategic management should instead be an embedded exercise incorporating input from both staff and management. Strategic teams should be seen as permanent and positive agents of change rather than unwelcomed hired guns who come in to disrupt organisations every once in a while.

After all strategic execution requires continual engagement and cross-functional collaboration to make it work. It should not be perceived as some one-off, dark magic conjured up and delivered every three to five years.

Strategy in today's operating climate

To recap what strategy isn't, here are the three items to ensure do *not* occur when practicing strategic management:

1. *Creating a strategy without an achievable vision*

2. *Performing the art of strategy as a fragmented exercise*

3. *Strategy as a one-off process done every 3 or 5 years*

Though it may sound a bit negative saying what not to do, each of these points help to articulate context, intent and approach to strategy. It's an attempt to parameterise the nature of strategy without trying to define it.

And perhaps this is all anyone really needs to know. Joseph Joubert's quote at the beginning of the chapter gives me reassurance that strategic value can be explained without seeking a 'holy-grail' definition to something historically hard to pinpoint.

So what do these rules tell us? What additional insights can we learn from them? When looking at the boundaries of what strategy isn't, we can conceptualise strategy into two essential elements – strategic thinking (rule 1) and strategic enablement (rules 2 and 3).

These rules are intertwined and cannot be done without consideration for the others. Therefore, strategic thinking cannot be done in isolation without strategic enablement an active part in that process.

Conceptually I'd like to think strategic thinking is simply a state of mind requiring only the need to have a creative, innovative mindset. Strategic enablement on the other hand is the analytical, or opposing side, which questions the creative. It asks first if the vision is achievable and if so, how can we best get there with the least disruption and greatest return as possible.

I've often heard if the art of strategy is simply about continuous improvement planning for the organisation. In today's business disruptive climate this wouldn't apply. Rule 2 negates the practice of performing operational efficiencies, a differing approach to organisational planning.

Michael Porter writes that operational effectiveness can "eliminate wasted effort, employ more advanced technology, motivate employees better, or have greater insight into managing particular activities or sets of activities (Porter, Kim and Mauborgne 2011, 3)." It's a powerful argument. Yet he also warns those that only seek this path, as "the pursuit of operational effectiveness is seductive because it is concrete and actionable (Porter, Kim and Mauborgne 2011, 29)." It may be seductive and actionable, but it does not guarantee company future success.

So performing operational efficiencies is about achieving individual activity excellence, remaining competitive through continuous improvements, and being risk-agnostic in some ways. Conversely, strategic management is about combining a multitude of business activities, taking known risks and making tough choices through an evidence-based approach. They are both essential to a business's growth plans but work quite differently.

Think of a two-sided planning coin as pictured below. One side is dedicated to strategic growth whilst the other to operational efficiencies.

Organisational Planning Coin:
Knowing the differences

Strategic Value	Operational Efficiency Value
Competitive Edge / Growth	Mimic Competition / Stay in the Game

Many organisations will flip this coin only once in the air, usually landing heads up on operational efficiency value. Over an extended period of time, this can be detrimental to an organisation as it encourages a business silo pursuit. It is a situation whereby each line of business chooses to independently optimise their own business to meet their own goals. The longer the coin stays face up, the greater the risk these silos begin to work against the organisation.

Organisations can quickly lose sight of again flipping the coin to ensure strategy value is also pursued. Failing to strategically plan is planning to fail. It is important to acknowledge the two sides need to co-exist and to know each of their boundaries within all organisations.

Knowing when and how often to flip the coin is the trick to performing effective organisational planning. The larger the organisation, the more thought should be given to this question.

With the boundaries of strategy discussed, it's time to investigate a set of new strategic imperatives that have become key to organisational success.

PART B:

Our New Strategic Imperatives

CHAPTER 4:

The Value of All Things Human

"Love and work are the cornerstones of our humanness."

– Sigmund Freud

Why include a chapter that is founded on elements of sociology and anthropology? Business strategy is not only about financial rewards, business processes and management structures; it is also very much about people and culture. As the rate and pace of change continues to accelerate, many senior executives and board directors have traditionally underestimated these imperatives when developing and executing their strategic initiatives.

I do wonder if we honestly try and engender a better workplace for ourselves. A workplace we can be proud to come to work each day. I'm reminded of a scene from 'Joe Versus the Volcano', starring Tom Hanks. (What a wonderful actor!) Tom's character, Joe, is working in the basement of this fictional company. There are rows of florescent lights with sparse and dilapidated office furniture. Together with his unappreciative boss, the entire setting is the worst work environment imaginable. He often gets sick, visibly pale and white in the face. Not one of his co-workers cracks a smile; each minding his or her business. It's a bleak picture indeed.

Until recently, understanding what truly makes each of us happy has been largely overlooked in the workplace. The study of 'why we do the things we do' is what I refer to as the study of our human condition. It's an area that has fascinated me for decades. Socrates once said "It is not living that matters, but living rightly."

Take for example the concept of change in the workplace. For many of us, change is something we don't look forward to. Whether it's procrastination, fear of having to perform something different, or fear of the unknown, many of us tend to delay the change as long as possible. In doing so, we are potentially making that change more disruptive for ourselves—the change event becomes a bigger deal than it has to. At a deeper level this may explain why we prefer settling into communities of like-minded people, rather than having to always move from place to place.

From a business point of view, sudden change in direction or cultural (for example as a result of a merger) can be quite disruptive and in cases, disastrous. The risk of not being able to deliver qualitative goods and services exponentially increase for the organisation. There is even a risk that the company may not survive the onslaught of the change.

One way to lessen the risk of disruptive change is to practice strategic management. Planning activities can identify changes up front and ensure they occur with some orderly fashion. Doing so will also reduce shareholder and community-related concerns about a business's direction and purpose. In an indirect way, publishing a strategic plan can act as a positive recruitment vehicle attracting like-minded people to join the company.

This chapter explores a set of humanistic tendencies applicable to our working lives. Understanding these tendencies can create better strategic approaches to overcoming a host of business challenges.

Hunter-gatherers versus communes

Some dozen years ago I started to think that people could easily be identified as falling into two simple buckets. What I termed at the time, hunter-gatherers and communes.

I cannot honestly remember what triggered this thought. Nevertheless, I just couldn't shake this idea in the months to come.

By nature, hunter-gatherers are always on the go, eager to explore the next mystery around the corner. They are the adventurers and thrill seekers as well as society's non-conformists. They are also the minority amongst us.

For hunter-gatherers the notion of change is a constant and a given. This is what fuels their lifestyle. They have the ability to become great storytellers; many of us gravitate to them for inspiration. They need not be extroverts, but they are the ones we like to read about.

Conversely, communes enjoy certainty; they cope better when they better understand the environment they live in. Everyone has a role and a place. Most of us are communes and generally are risk averse to change. So fierce is the inherit nature to resist it that us communes wait until the last minute to accept the change.

If someone were to ask the percentage makeup of these two groups, I would propose (without any empirical evidence other than from my own experiences) about ten to fifteen percent of people are hunter-gatherers at any one point in time. It is nearly impossible to prove because people can, and do indeed, switch between the two groups. For example, many of us find the thrill of adventure in our early twenties, myself included. As we get older we tend to become more communal. However we should never belong to both at the same time. It's awfully hard to try and be both and keep a sane outlook on life.

How then does this relate to the book? For many of us much of what we do at work is routine and repetitive. Our personal lives may mirror our work environment as well – return home, say hello to the family, feed the kids and have dinner, bath time, homework, watch a little television, chat a bit and then off to bed.

We tend to shy away from changes being introduced to our working environment, especially if we see them as big changes. There's also degree of anxiety to them.

Studies have shown that our brain likes to hardwire repetitive tasks by storing these tasks into a deeper region of the brain that doesn't require as much 'thinking energy'. Tasks become easier to do once they are hardwired into the brain. Conscious thought, on the other hand, occupies a different area of the brain that requires a heavy dose of thinking. The result is more neural pathways are connected. This requires larger amounts of energy consumption for our brain. That is why thinking is simply harder to do.

Change by nature is not repetitive. It can be daunting as it forces us to think about the rationale of the change and how this change will affect our day-to-day work. When we first learn of the change our brain is using higher amounts of energy and working harder. Feelings of anxiousness, nervousness, and even dread, can quickly descend upon us. Fear of the unknown can take root as a result.

So if we are so susceptible to change affecting our working environment, then why do so many businesses perform so poorly with change? Due to the competitive nature of businesses, many tend to immediately throw change upon their employees, unprepared for the potential ripple it can have on the organisation. Some businesses are better able to cope with change than others. It simply comes down to being more organised and prepared for when and how the change will occur.

In today's faster pace working environment, business change is happening more frequently and at quicker rates than ever before. So there's a natural tension between the communes' sense of security knowing where things stand juxtaposed to the reality of the working world of today. Finding solutions for how to manage change is becoming a top business priority in the quest to either stay competitive, or perhaps leapfrog the competition entirely.

This concept of sudden organisational change is something I wrote about in my master's thesis in the early 1990s. It was a work entitled, 'Environmental ACIDs' (Accidents, Crisis', Incidents, and Disasters). Using an evidence-based approach, the paper demonstrated how large and complex organisations, be they commercial businesses or government agencies, failed to effectively manage fast-moving and highly volatile environmental situations.

To better respond to these headline-grabbing situations, I argued for a global emergency readiness system built around agility and flexibility. A system structured, above all else, for responding quickly to a situation rather than a system whose priority was to remain permanently viable.

I believe the same logic can be applied in the current business climate. Simply replace 'volatile environmental situations' with 'technology disruptions' as the agent of change. Replace 'large and complex organisations' with 'out-of-date vertical management structures'. Technology disruptions are today having an enormous impact on older management structures that cannot cope with the continuing and quickening forces of change.

The result is higher levels of un-happiness at work than ever before. We need to rethink our approach to those communes who help create the value our businesses deliver. Doing so will unlock hidden value trapped within the business. Interesting enough, the answer may lie with those hunter-gatherers who can teach us a thing or two about living on the edge.

What matters to us?

To better understand what makes each of us tick, we need a deeper dive into the human condition. Whether we are communes or hunter-gatherers, we each have a set of common traits we all live by.

What motivates each of us, and how do we each manage to cope and survive in our environment? Much academic work has already been conducted here. I'm personally interested in a few key traits that affect how we work, or when we conduct a business transaction.

In trying to understand what motivates people, the well-known psychologist Abraham Maslow once said, "The story of the human race is the story of men and women selling themselves short (Pursuit of Happiness n.d.)." In 1943 he introduced his now famous 'hierarchy of needs', a model that describes how one can attain gratitude and life satisfaction.

Over the years Maslow improved upon the model culminating in his 1954 book, *Motivation and Personality*. He described a five-layer approach in which the first four layers support the top layer, self-actualisation. He argued that an individual cannot achieve this top layer without first satisfying the bottom four.

Though there are critics of Maslow, his theory today retains many merits. Though he never used a pyramid to illustrate his hierarchy of needs, it is usually represented this way. So in the spirit of pyramid building, I present my own version to highlight three work-related concepts we will explore in this section.

Maslow's Hierarchy of Needs Applied to the Workplace

Self-actualisation

Esteem — Accomplishment

Love / Belonging — Altruism

Safety — Job Security

Physiological

WORK-RELATED CONCEPTS

To better understand motivation, coping and surviving at work, let's look at these three work-related items: the nature of job security, the concept of altruism and the sense of accomplishment. Each sits at a different layer of the hierarchy, and each item uniquely challenges our traditional way of thinking about the workplace. I'll take a bottom up approach in exploring them. First up, job security.

In Maslow's model, job security aligns to the 'safety' layer. Other items that Maslow called out on the same level are health and personal security. In another words, security in our environment or job security is considered a more basic need than relationships (which reside on the love and belonging layer).

Taking away someone's job is no doubt, a traumatic event for the individual concerned. It's akin to removing one's safety blanket, like being stripped naked and thrown off a plane flying over Antarctica. Perhaps I'm not painting the best visual here; however, for many in that situation, it may feel very much like that.

The second workplace need is the concept of altruism. This need aligns to the Love and Belonging layer. At first glance it may not sound like a natural fit for our working environment, but I believe altruism is a very underrated force in our lives.

The debate around altruism is the age-old question of whether we are naturally born altruistic or are conditioned by our environment to become altruistic. I read a book during my undergraduate days that argued there are plenty of cases where hardened criminals, given a sudden opportunity to save someone's life, did indeed attempt to save that life in nearly every case. I'm also struck by how newborn babies exude a sense of good and happiness within us. It's as if we return to a time of innocence, a place where a ray of sunshine and 'anything is possible' seem to be imprinted on that baby's face.

The evidence I've read leads me to be a believer that all of us are born altruistic, and we subconsciously return to this condition when faced with witnessing birth or life-threatening situations. How then can this powerful and natural drug be harnessed within the working environment? Shouldn't it be on the mind of our leaders and strategic management teams when considering change or finding that next inspirational moment?

Nothing breaks down barriers like a genuine smile. It is a fantastic disarming tool against people who have put up their protective walls. Think of the power of adopting a genuine smile at work each and every day. Work is the place where we spend approximately seventy percent of our waking days. The ability to integrate altruism at work can dramatically increase performance and remove those business silos. It's a powerful concept we'll revisit when exploring the important virtues of leadership.

The third and final work-related need is a sense of accomplishment. In a world where we are constantly bombarded by information, are expected to take on multiple and varied tasks each day, and are forever reminded of things we need to get done, it is becoming harder to feel any accomplishment about the things we do. This 'busyness' can ultimately affect our self-esteem, the layer just below self-actualisation. A recently debuted book elegantly captures this on its back cover:

> *Today's world is one of too much: too much work to do, too much communication, too much competition, too much uncertainty and too much information. We are striving to keep up, but inevitably we're falling behind, leaving us with a nagging sense of failure that is hard to shake off. It's unsustainable commercially, draining professionally, depressing personally. It's not much fun (Crabbe 2014).*

Left untreated, busyness can lead to higher levels of stress and begin to affect our confidence levels. It also affects how others may begin to perceive us, weakening and eroding away our physiological sense of purpose or accomplishment.

An article I read some time ago classified various levels of stressful moments and rated them from one to ten, where ten was most stressful. At ten were things such as a death in the family, marriage, divorce, and the birth of children. Near the bottom were minor nuisances like someone's annoying ring tone, having a bad traffic morning, and being late to a work meeting.

What struck me were the reaction people exhibited for things that were classified as being one or two. A good example the article quoted is road rage—a clear and over-the-top reaction to getting stuck in traffic. It should theoretically not cause a great amount of stress.

If our emotional levels are running high due to stress build-up, it can greatly affect our ability to think clear and rationally. One approach to combat stress levels is to practice being 'mindful' which can keep us sharp mentally when we start to feel too busy.

Being mindful is the ability to see our own emotions, thoughts and sensations so that we can make better and more informed choices. Mindfulness is a virtue of the human condition. Techniques such as the use of mediation and action-based exercises can assist in achieving a state of mindfulness.

Why not encourage management teams to practice mindfulness? One leader I recently reported to would set aside ten minutes before the start of our weekly team meeting to practice meditation, or in his words 'clear the mind'. This may sound a bit odd to many readers (and indeed it was strange for me at first), but we quickly moved past the awkwardness and were able to clear our minds.

Depending on the day or week, some of us were more stressed than others. The 'clear the mind' session allowed us to reset and start our meeting from a common and relaxed mental state.

The result was a more constructive session driving higher collaborative and qualitative decision-making outcomes. Individually we all felt a greater sense of accomplishment was achieved in the process. Secondly, it brought our management team closer together via a regular and social-bond experience (more on that in the following section).

As time passed we were even asked to take turns in leading the mindfulness session. Ultimately the team developed into one of the highest performing groups in the organisation as demonstrated through our organisation-wide performance ratings.

Another approach to achieving a higher sense of accomplishment is managing our time better. Today endless streams of email, text messages and tweets constantly bombard us. Holding a lunch conversation without being interrupted by our mobility device is harder and harder to achieve. For many of us we are in a constant state of digital overload.

Within the office environment, the situation is worse. A survey conducted in March 2011 by the market research firm uSamp found that "many employees are interrupted at least every 15 minutes, and the majority waste at least an hour a day dealing with all types of distractions. And when each of those distractions happens, it can take 20 minutes to regain focus and get back to the work at hand (Cohen 2011)." Four years on from this survey, I wonder how much that 15 minutes has shrunk to.

I'd like to share two tips to better time management that has allowed me to better cope and be less busy. One I call 'meeting avoidance' and the other, 'time creation'.

In terms of meeting avoidance, it works on the principle of only attending any subject-matter meetings that are outcome based. When faced with a meeting invite that does not state its aims or objectives then do a 'tentative' RSVP and ask to know what the meeting is about. If no explanation is forthcoming before the meeting takes place, it is a valid excuse to not show up.

The second tip I can share is time creation, or carving out time where none seems to exist. It's about blocking off free time in advance into one's calendar. This time could be labelled as 'work time' in the diary entry. It is time allocated to the 'doing side' of the job. And it's the doing side that best brings out our sense of accomplishment.

Think of it this way. We all mark time in our calendars to agree to discuss and meet with each other, so why not mark time to ensure we also perform the work that is asked of us?

Both these tips saved my sanity within a high pressure-cooker government management role. It was a role in which I worked late nearly every day to accomplish the work I could not accomplish during normal working hours. I found myself slowly sinking, never able to catch up on the past several days of work. I felt like I was accomplishing very little to show what I was capable of.

My stress levels markedly increased. I became more abrupt in my communication patterns, and was continually frustrated at nearly everything that came across my desk. I was that road-rage guy waiting to happen. When I started working throughout some weekends, I knew it was time to change something. So I put both tips into practice.

The ensuing results were phenomenal. By attending fewer meetings and blocking off some additional time for myself, I could perform higher quality work during normal business hours.

In that particular role I was a crucial stakeholder to a number of project managers. By freeing up my time from attending meetings, I became more available to those project managers to help them make quick, informative decisions. It wasn't just me that benefited but also other parts of the organisation as well. I then encouraged my own team to practice the same thing, and many accepted the challenge.

It is all about working smarter instead of harder. An effective time management strategy together with regular mindfulness exercises is a powerful combination to combat the busyness. In turn we are rewarded with a greater sense of accomplishment. Our levels of confidence and self-esteem are preserved and strengthened.

So how would these three work-related needs fit into a strategic management plan? Here is one interpretation.

When thinking about transforming a business, there will be individuals who will be asked to leave the organisation and others who will be asked to take on different roles. Ensuring a dignified approach for each affected individual is paramount to a successful transition. The strategic plan also needs to ensure an altruistic approach that provides high levels of inspiration and camaraderie. Lastly, the approach should consider the workload of staff. Maintain or create a working environment conducive to a sense of accomplishment for each employee by targeting areas that contribute to high levels of busyness.

In conclusion, being aware of these three work-related needs can lay the foundation of building more effective workplaces. Maslow discussed the importance of dignity and self-fulfilment as attributes that belong in the hierarchy of needs highest layer, self-actualisation. In essence, the three work-related needs act as support anchors for these two. It is about getting the basics right and performing them repeatedly. Doing so will allow us to attain a sense of dignity and self-fulfilment within our work places.

What do we look for in others?

Our interaction with each other is just as important as how we individually view ourselves.

In my mid 30s I found myself single and without many close friends. Most of these friends were married, and the vast majority had kids. As life would dictate, they settled into new social circles mostly with others that were married with children.

Finding a new set of like-minded single friends who were of the similar age proved quite challenging until I stumbled across an advertisement for a new social club. The concept sounded brilliant and for me it was a chance to meet like-minded people. I immediately signed up and paid my membership subscription. After attending various social events I found it easy to meet new people and develop friendships in the process.

The social club did not disappoint. It delivered what it promised. It matched my expectations to the quality service I expected. Other club members I talked to also had similar experiences. The club succeeded in making it much easier to create social bonds between strangers.

The desire to *socially connect and build a bond* with each other is a strong force. I believe it's inherent within each of us, written in our

DNA. Some people need heavier doses of it than others, but each of us needs it at some level.

This desire extends into our workplaces and it can be quite telling. Though at times each of us may feel socially isolated at work (perhaps due to geographic, language or even self-imposed working barriers), it doesn't take long before others start to worry about us. There is usually an inherit pull by a particular someone, or perhaps by a group of work colleagues, to bring us closer to our working communities.

But it is not just about reconnecting from feeling isolated. Those that tend to succeed in a business environment tend to have higher doses of social connectedness.

This is not about being extrovert over introvert either. I know many successful leaders who avoid big public scenes, preferring one-on-one exchanges with staff. They are the quiet achievers who enjoy connecting with people. Bonding with people leads to trust. It is an essential trait for any successful business relationship.

By getting to know work colleagues, we discover and gain an appreciation of their values and moral compass. There is an innate need to better understand people we are drawn to. It not only bonds us but also makes us feel better about ourselves. It reinforces our own sense of identity.

Another desirable trait we look for in others is the *perception of being organised*. This has less to do with someone begin reactive versus proactive. It refers to whether someone simply appears to be 'with it', or confident and relaxed. Can they anticipate the next move and appear to have everything under control?

I studied political science for my graduate work, and I'd like to use an analogy related to democratic political systems. Contrary to popular belief a large percentage of people tend to vote based on the perception of whether one leader is more organised than the other. Yes, some voters will indeed cast their vote based on a particular issue. This is especially true if it is a life altering decision or they feel incredibly passionate about it, but often voters do not fall into either of these extremes.

Let me illustrate election campaign tactics to describe the perception of being organised. Attack ads are designed to throw off an opponent to see how they react (or don't) to that attack. The attack ad may be on a particular issue or set of issues but it is designed as a character assassination.

If the candidate defends the attack well and appears relatively unharmed by it, then there's a perception they must be well organised. Alternatively, if the attack if effective and they don't defend effectively, then the candidate's poll rating usually drops as a consequence.

Let's say an attack is about a candidate's behavioural traits. If the candidate differs in response to what was said from his or her election team, the attacks will continue on this topic. They are meant to try and divide the candidate from the team and thereby weaken his or her organisational leadership capabilities. The voting community will begin to question the 'strength' of this candidate.

There are many famous examples to cite from past Presidential U.S. elections, including the first televised debate debacle of Nixon versus Kennedy; the 'read my lips, no new taxes' pledge of George Bush (senior); and the repeated attack campaigns on Bill Clinton's womanising during his first run to the White House. Each of these attacks by the opposing party was aimed at weakening the resolve of the candidate – to portray them as being incapable of leading a nation.

The first two, in the examples above, worked to dislodge the front-runner; the last didn't. Some would argue, that the attacks on Bill Clinton had the opposite effect, as he seemed to easily deflect everything that was thrown at him during the presidential campaign. It strengthened his leadership credentials.

This election tactic is generally not effective on voters who are on the extreme end of the political spectrum. It is not meant to, but aims to persuade mainstream voters who are not entrenched within a political party platform.

In another words political issues are just the battleground, but not the battle itself. The battle is ultimately for voters' hearts and minds. Here a voter's heart represents the emotionally side (perception) and the voter mind represents whether the candidate is in fact organised.

The same line of argument applies in our working environment. We are employees (voters) who are trying to determine whether we trust our leaders to make our working environment better for us. Those who do not appear organised will have to work harder for our vote of confidence.

A third and final observation is that many of us would prefer others to not preach or tell us what to do. It's largely seen as a poor behaviour trait. We'd rather *associate with those who provide implicit support and guidance* without telling us how to do things.

Immigration agents, professionals who represent a migrant's case for resettlement, have to perform this skill well. They are the representative between the migrant and the state official processing the immigration visa.

The practice of immigration law can be murky at times. It requires a well-versed agent to not only keep abreast to changes in the law, but also to navigate the idiosyncrasies of a particular case he or she is representing. An agent would never choose to argue with a state official about who is right or wrong. It might jeopardise the case itself. It is better to guide that state official to their point of view without telling them. It is a fine art indeed.

Managers are often associated with telling people what to do whilst leaders are often associated with inspiring their peers to excel. Those that inspire others generally avoid making assumptions about peoples' behaviours and interactions.

What does this mean for strategists? In earlier decades, strategists might have pontificated from an ivory tower, assuming too many things along the way. In today's evidence-based business climate, strategists should not assume anything. They should escape the creature comforts of the ivory tower.

Strategists require greater degrees of connectedness with the people they represent. In another words strategists should focus less on reacting to and managing situations, and instead spend more effort becoming leaders who in turn inspire heads of.

To illustrate an example, one of aims of a strategist is to enable conversation to ultimately seek endorsement for a strategic plan or action. The trick is to show someone the path without telling them how to walk it. It's that fine line between describing the answer without actually providing the answer to someone. This, I believe, is one of the most difficult things to master but one of the most valuable skills to possess.

Yesterday's strategic management practices tended to be mechanical, specialising on principally financial and investment performance. In a social media fuelled world where communities are resetting the boundaries to profitability, today's strategic management practices require a new approach on how to interact with work colleagues and leaders.

In recapping what we seek from others, a strategist needs to consider a) the importance of building relationships founded on inclusiveness and respect, b) the importance of being organised in the eyes of others, and c) adopting a communication style meant to inspire rather than control situations.

The value in empowerment and curiosity

How often does your organisation consider its decision-making and management style and find better ways to govern itself? Although this subject matter continues to be well covered in self-help literature, poor decision-making and management styles continue to remain an ever-present obstacle for many businesses today. Has management not applied any techniques from all those self-help books on the market? What's really going on here?

A long-standing area of interest of mine has been the difference between management and a directorship. I believe making the move from a senior manager to a director is perhaps one of the most challenging job transitions to make in a business career.

Most managers getting promoted to a director are ill prepared to take on such a different role. Much of the reason is because these two roles require completely different skill sets. Managers are most effective at running operations. Directors are most effective as good planners who set the future operational parameters for their management teams.

While this may appear as a subtle difference on paper, for many it is a chasm that requires significant re-orientation of one's mindset. The chasm forces a manager to change their historical decision-making approach and style.

Often managers are forced to react to operational situations. They are largely measured (and perceived) on how they handle these unforeseen circumstances. Yet, managers are rarely measured on how well they planned for situations that never eventuated.

As a manager for most of my career I can never recall a performance metric measuring how well I planned for 'the unknowns'. On the contrary I was often asked in my annual review to discuss how well I managed those unforeseen situations in avoiding the situation from being escalated.

I'm not trying to diminish the value of those reviews. They were of sound merit to ensuring I performed well in managing situations. However, those reviews did not prepare me for a career to becoming a director.

Directors on the other hand are largely responsible in setting business targets and direction. They have performance indicators aligned, for example, to business efficiencies and revenue generation. Naturally they are asked from time to time to handle an escalated operational issue or two, but that is not their primary purpose. Directors are more like a ship's captain. The managers are his or her ship's duty officers.

So if a set of managers has a habit of escalating nearly every operational issue, that director will have very little time to think about the future state of the business. Instead, he or she will become consumed with operational efficiencies to fix operational weaknesses. There's a trap here.

Avoiding this director trap has more to do with sociology than with business governance. It's about making a mental shift that allows managers to own those situations. More specifically it is about empowering managers that they have what it takes to succeed.

Think about the current crop of directors in your organisation. Which ones were promoted internally? Of those, which were taught this empowerment philosophy before being promoted?

If directors spent more time performing planning activities, they stand a better chance of increasing morale from those who work under them. Those under their direction will better understand their landscape and feel more comfortable about their own role within that landscape. There will be a greater sense of trust and accountability between everyone.

And like a sea captain guiding the ship, the duty officers will feel better knowing their destination and where difficult challenges may lie. They each will be better informed to work out on their own the how and when in performing their roles.

In summary, *empowering managers to manage situations* allows directors more time to focus on the *future* of their business. Doing so will trigger a greater sense of *curiosity across the business group.*

When I moved to Australia many years ago, I met a memorable taxi driver who drove me to Denver airport. What struck me were not necessarily the specifics of our discussion but his curiosity about me, as well as mine about him. Prior to his many years as a taxi driver, he had migrated to Denver from Ethiopia.

He went on to explain how his curiosity allowed him to better make sense of situations. It allowed him to rationalise not only his understanding about his new country of residence, but also his ability to identify with strangers. Curiosity allowed him to adapt to various social conversations in a country quite different culturally to the one he grew up in.

We chatted until I arrived at the airport. When I mentioned that I could locate Ethiopia on a world map and knew it had been through a recent civil war, he said my awareness of his homeland was enough to make his day.

Our mutual curiosity allowed us to leave our prejudices behind, and open ourselves to learning more. We both expanded our minds in the process. A quote from Socrates couldn't be more poignant. "True knowledge exists in knowing that you know nothing."

The opposite of curiosity is critique. If a business plan from a director is put forth without some degree of staff participation or involvement, then lack of consent will open the door to criticism and ultimately dissent. This is the glass half empty scenario.

If, on the other hand, a director is transparent and affords their people an opportunity to contribute, then the team is much more likely to be engaged and supportive. The opportunity to contribute also creates a communication channel, potentially bringing fresh ideas to the table. Again empowerment has to be there, a glass half full scenario.

Employees' who have their performance goals aligned to those of the organisation are more willing to work with strategies in place. They feel connected to the greater good and a sense of purpose in their roles. Ensuring alignment of performance goals can significantly reduce employee resistance in adopting a new direction or business outcomes.

Obviously developing a culture founded on curiosity rather than criticism can take time. The journey starts at the top of management totem pole. It starts with both directors and managers practicing empowerment to build trust and confidence across their teams.

Some of you reading this might be thinking 'why doesn't he discuss the 'L' word?' And you are right in recognising that what lies beneath the concepts of empowerment and curiosity is leadership.

One of my favourite reads is *Quiet Leadership: Six Steps to Transforming Performance at Work* by David Rock. His book describes how a leader can reorient their thinking to then resetting their emotions and behaviours. The book teaches directors and managers to stop *thinking for people* and; instead, help *people think for themselves*.

A book about business strategy cannot be written without a discussion on leadership, which I'll take up later in the book.

Revisiting the importance of an organisation's cultural identity

In the early 1990s while researching my master's thesis, I came across a book by Edgar Schein called *Organizational Culture and Leadership*. First released in 1985, today the book is considered one of the most influential management books there is.

It described the value of people as a competitive advantage. What made it unique was that it was written from an anthropological background and considered, at that time, quite ground breaking research. It was published at a time when the Kaizen philosophy dominated the business landscape.

The model Edgar put forth is simple and elegant. He described each organisation as having three basic cultural layers: an outer layer called 'artefacts', a middle 'espoused values' layer and the inner core layer defined as 'assumptions'. Artefacts are the visible side of culture and can be anything from the office furniture to the organisational chart, along with its business processes. Espoused values are things like a corporate vision, strategies, philosophies and business principles. Finally, there are the underlying assumptions that reflect the organisation's set of shared values. These are largely based on the human condition, and can include culturally ethnic or country-to-country differences.

As an example, Australian culture tends to exhibit more passive resistance than one may expect from other Western countries. This behaviour is a change inhibitor that may be difficult to detect for those not familiar with this cultural nuance.

For companies with offices spread around the world, these variances in country assumptions can slightly alter the layer above it, the espoused values, from office to office. To avoid cultural confusion and frustration, any global change program needs to account for these disparate assumptions found deep within the organisation. Underlying assumptions and espoused values both require constant nurturing and attention to prevent organisational cultural erosion. The risk of not performing this can result in an organisation lacking a moral compass and thereby producing inefficiencies.

Edgar's three layers can be thought of like an onion. When you peel back the layers, you get closer to the inner core. The core ultimately affects the outlying layers.

The underlying assumptions resemble in form and function how humans behave and interact. To put it another way, the organisation is founded on how people behave and interact. After all, an organisation is made up of groups of people interacting with each other.

Returning back to my thesis research, I remember pondering whether an organisation was simply an extension of our humanistic tendencies or something that was more complex and unique. Edgar's book shaped my thinking and appreciation about the essence of an organisation. The ability for an organisation to change direction or what it stands for starts and stops with its people.

We often think of change management as a fairly recent field of study; and it is, but not without precedent. In fact, the field was borne out of the theory and thinking behind organisational development some thirty-odd years ago. The thinking about an organisation's unique culture is only two decades younger than the field of strategic management. Today the field once known as organisational development is going through a recent renaissance, and two major forces underpin it.

First, the business world is reshaping itself to a customer-led one. It is moving away from a delivery-dominated world of new product tweaks, features and who is more efficient at making them. The quest to understand customer behaviours and loyalty has forced management to once again revisit the importance of organisational culture. If employees are happy so will our customers be.

The second force is within the field itself. Many academics are exploring at deeper levels the insights affecting the human condition. The academic community is gaining a deeper appreciation of how we operate and function in society. These new insights are finding their way into the business landscape.

Societal value and conscious choices

There is something innate in all of us to want to do good for others, those altruistic notions explored earlier. For example, we feel better about where we work when our employer is seen as contributing to the betterment of society. It may be from donating a lump sum of money to a charitable cause, or perhaps publically championing a common cause.

Regrettably a number of organisations do not adequately tap into this wellspring of 'do-good' opportunities. Imagine that by better tapping into this well, businesses could actually expand their operations and become more profitable. This scenario is a quasi-utopia; a perfect marriage between employee, employer and society at large.

One industry is achieving this very thing. They are the Not For Profits, or NFPs. These organisations have traditionally delivered positive value back to the communities they service, but have historically struggled for a way to effectively measure the community value they provide.

Traditional ways to measure NFP success were in the form of growth metrics such as membership numbers, marketing reach and penetration. The only way to demonstrate community value was to intangibly promote this through various promotional channels and documented case studies of what they achieved.

There simply was no visible and direct way to measure actual and repeatable value being delivered to the communities they serve. It's a quandary. How do organisations like this measure the social value they are most known for? Does someone try and count the number of times a client smiles each day?

Thankfully a number of community-minded organisations have started measuring the social value they deliver. One such industry is Aged Care, and it's currently witnessing a massive transformation on a global scale. The industry is being asked to provide more targeted and specific provisioning of care for the individual.

Traditional nursing homes are being replaced with in-home care and assisted community living models. New models of care, such as 'person-centred care' (PCC) and 'consumer-driven care' (CDC), are gaining attention to address these new societal pressures. These models are founded on many of Maslow's needs hierarchy such as safety, security, compassion, spiritual growth, and wellbeing.

There are two major forces impacting upon this massive industry transformation: baby boomers and new governmental pressures on financial stewardship.

In numerous western countries, the baby boomer generation is not only living longer than previous generations before it, it also has a larger population (thanks to the population explosion following World War II). This generation has seen plenty of wealth creation and now is looking forward to retirement to take advantage of that created wealth. It is not surprising that many baby boomers would prefer to stay at home and age gracefully rather than be put into a nursing home. To be able to live at home requires that they live healthier for longer.

The size of the baby boomer's population, the wealth they created for themselves, and the ability to live longer than their parents present a unique set of challenges for national governments. Just the sheer number of baby boomers can significantly strain many of these existing health systems.

Governments with a high population of baby boomers are in support of this 'home care' or 'assisted living' position. The case being that it will lessen their total cost of caring for the baby boom generation as it reduces the need for them to be supported by the existing national health system.

The second major transforming force in Aged Care is outsourcing of government social services. The Global Financial Crisis, and in particular, what resulted afterwards, has seen many governments take on higher levels of debt to cover the 'too big to fail' businesses.

To lessen taxpayer burdens and bring these debts under control, many governments have decided to significantly reduce or completely exit out of certain social services they have historically provided. In return, they look to for-profit and not-for-profit businesses to provide these social services. For a suitable price, businesses can opt to purchase the licence to provide these services. From a government perspective this not only eliminates operational costs, the selling price can immediately go into government coffers to pay down their public debts.

However, many governments are requiring as part of the outsourcing transaction that these businesses regularly report and comply with their service standards from a common set of business measurements. Business outcomes are then used by these government agencies to track the business performance of their outsourced social services. In turn, governments are seen to doing the right thing for their taxpayer base whilst minimising costs.

The challenge for this outsourced model is how to measure social and individual return on something that was not historically measured when it was managed by the government. Previously, government agencies ran these services as 'output' generating services, or services that simply showed progress (not necessarily results) to the greater communities they served.

For those NFP organisations that wish to take on these government services, this outcome-based business model is something quite new. It is a major culture shift. So back to the earlier question of how does an organisation measure social value?

Luckily there are already good models finding their way into mainstream use. The models are based on a widely accepted concept called Social Return On Investment, or SROI. They are supported in business practice through a 'social benefit', or SB framework. (I'll examine the importance of a framework a bit later.) The SB provides the rules of the road in regards to how to define and measure value.

The actual value measurements, or instruments, are called things like social impact bonds (SIB), or alternatively, social benefit bonds (SBB). These instruments are currently being adopted between government agencies and NFPs in diverse places like the United Kingdom, Canada, Japan, the United States and Australia.

Each instrument is based on a reward-based mechanism for providing funding; prove that the SB has been delivered and the bond will grant additional funds. Each may be constructed differently depending on the terms and conditions of the SB service contract. This is an exciting and fundamentally new frontier to demonstrate business value and growth for NFPs, offering great promise.

The Aged Care sector is just one example of how social value is being captured. Many other organisations are finding ways to develop and support social value.

Pro Bono Australia is a good case study. An online organisation dedicated to connecting a range of not-for-profit charities, the group has also setup a corporate community initiative to help for-profit businesses engage in community development work. They state, "Increasingly, corporations are motivated to become more socially responsible because their stakeholders expect them to understand and address social and community issues that are relevant to them (Pro Bono Australia 2014)."

This begs the question of what is a socially conscious business? Though there are many definitions, I like to summarise it as embedding values based on social and environmental concerns into the DNA of a business. There are now a number of global movements supporting these types of businesses. A few are Conscious Capitalism, the B-Team and B Corps. These groups all have one thing in common: Putting purpose into profit by supporting a corporate socially responsible platform (CSR).

These new social models are there for the taking when considering a competitive advantage. Think of a horse derby. Many corporate organisations have already bolted out of their CSR gates. Is your organisation still stuck in the gate or worse still, grazing in the paddock?

What does all of this have to do with strategic value?

As previously illustrated, strategy is not about performing a set of operational efficiencies to stay ahead of the competition. To achieve real growth in today's business climate, strategists need more than a business process rulebook.

A business's ability to quickly adapt to changes in the ever-shifting consumer driven world demands strategic attention. Understanding the customer experience, or a customer's interaction journey through a line of business, is absolutely fundamental to any competitive position.

A 2014 survey conducted by Optus found that just 45 percent of an organisation's decision-makers fully appreciate the impact customer experience has on their revenue and profits (SingTel Optus 2014, 9). Though there is plenty of talk about it, few are actually integrating the value of customer experience into their business' DNA. That is dangerous considering the business benefits are head turning.

The same survey found that those who deliver outstanding customer experience are *five* times more likely to retain loyal customers compared to those who provide average customer experience. Loyalty translates not only into retaining revenue it also creates business advocates. The survey found outstanding customer experience delivers *30 times* more advocates as those that are average (SingTel Optus 2014, 9). This is real growth!

To illustrate a real world example of effective customer experience value, I recount the success story of Aesop. Renowned for their premium skin, hair and body products, Aesop became a global giant through unconventional marketing. All their product packaging looks rather plain and dull. With the lone exception of the words on each label there is no clear distinction between their lines of product.

This was once considered suicide for any retail business in this space. Product image and the style in which they are packaged had always been the key competitive differentiators. To sell the value of their products Aesop instead focused on their customer's experience within each of their stores. At that time no competitor had attempted this.

They achieved this experience in two ways. First, they famously washed customer hands prior to any product trials, similar to washing our hands before we eat. They took extra care to washing in a soothing manner and used a nice, washable scent. Through an intimate touch and smell experience, their sales consultants were able to establish a closer bond with their customers. They connected in a more personal way.

Secondly Aesop augmented the customer experience by visually designing the front signage of each retail store to uniquely match the neighbourhood and its style. Each store physically looked like it belonged in that community, not apart from it.

Essentially they developed an immersive customer experience starting with the first sighting of the store, to the ambiance it represented and then to the personal, intimate attention each customer received. So different was their style and approach they were able to completely differentiate themselves from competitors. Aesop threw out the book to how they were *supposed* to compete. Instead, they innovated a new customer model from the ground up.

Their success speaks for itself. The company was sold to a Brazilian skincare competitor in December 2012 for a reported $68m. The deal included new capital to further expand their global reach. What better measure of success than to be acquired by a rival who guarantees additional cash to keep aggressively expanding the brand?

I should put in a cautionary note here, that there are plenty of ways to poorly capture and implement customer experiences. I personally have witnessed many organisations tackle customer experience only at the project level. If the project is delivered in isolation from other business groups, developing a customer experience can be misguided and fragmented, resulting in poor delivery decisions.

Customer experience value can also come from the wrong sources. Too often I have seen it discussed and decided in internal focus groups. This approach is completely backward. John Forsyth from McKinsey sums it up best.

> *"Focus groups are dead. If you're still using focus groups, you're using 30-year-old technology. A much better way to understand customer needs and behaviors is to spend time with people in their homes, stores, or health clubs. You watch them, you talk to them while they're doing the kinds of things we want to be observing (Gavett 2014)."*

In summary this chapter examined two humanistic models: Schein's organisational culture and Maslow's Needs Hierarchy. Though there are many other models in academia, the primary purpose is to show the practice of strategic management through a human kaleidoscope.

The success of businesses today requires a fairly robust humanistic approach to solving major organisational challenges. Need proof? Count the number of Chief Human Resources and Chief

Marketing Officers who now sit at the executive table, or even occupy a seat at the board level.

Want more proof? A recent Forbes article quoted the Talent Board that found 41% of job applicants search for information about an organisation's culture before they apply. Similar research from Bersin by Deloitte, in the same article, states that 95% of candidates believe culture is more important than compensation (Bersin 2015).

Culture will always trump strategy, unless culture is embedded into strategic thinking and performance outcomes. Thankfully culture can be more easily measured. These days there are dozens of cultural measurement tools emerging for mainstream businesses. Changes in culture begin from changes in employee behaviours and from organisational values that are espoused.

The business world is accelerating away from an emphasis on the next bells and whistles of a particular product to a world that concentrates first and foremost on the integrated role of the customer. For many businesses this is a major shift to make. Any business transformation will require new approaches to strategic management practices. Garry Emmons, writing an editorial piece about the book *Lords of Strategy*, best sums up this humanistic approach for strategic management.

> *"What the [human capital management] systems don't capture is Keynes's famous "animal spirits," entrepreneurial energies and imaginings that bring a business to life. They also miss out on the aspirations employees may harbor to think a bit on their own, experiment with new ways of doing the same old drill, and perhaps even be recognized by the company for what they create. For most of strategy's history, those are precisely the factors that the paradigm hasn't found a way to work into its calculations. If the [strategy] discipline is to continue to be of service, it will have to find that way (Emmons 2010)."*

A major reason for writing this book was to highlight this person-centric view of strategy. It's a world now full of business automation. We owe it to ourselves to challenge those antiquated business practices that attempt to devalue our human condition; to make us unhappy and disengaged at work. I use the excerpt below as a constant reminder when I roll out of bed and shuffle into the office.

human beings **are not computers**

We're not meant to run at high speeds, continuously, for long periods of time. Science tells us we're at our best when we move rhythmically between spending and renewing energy — a reality that companies must embrace to fuel sustainable engagement and high performance (The Energy Project 2015).

As technology becomes increasingly embedded into our working and personal lives, it becomes harder to distinguish our roles from a computer, or even a robot. So it's imperative to explore this technology paradigm as a great business disrupter.

CHAPTER 5:
The Rise and Rise of Technology

"Positioning – once the heart of strategy – is rejected as too static for today's dynamic markets and changing technologies. According to the new dogma, rivals can quickly copy any market position, and competitive advantage is, at best, temporary."

– Michael E Porter, "On Strategy", 2011

Though I have spent significant time in the technology industry if I were to make a choice between the value of people versus the value of technology, I would choose people 9 out of 10 times. In a perverse way I've learned it's rarely about the technology.

However, the fact remains so many people spend a great deal of time examining and discussing the value of a particular tech product or technology-centric solution. Part of the reason is that we are constantly bombarded by technology offerings everywhere we turn. It is near impossible to try and avoid it. No longer is technology a nice-to-have to become competitive. Those days are now long gone.

Technology is an imperative for both sides of the organisation's planning coin.

Yet with all this importance on technology, within the majority of organisations its strategic value still remains on the periphery of business strategy. Non-cost saving benefits from technology investments never get exposed to upper echelons of management. Too many times lower management use technology as a pawn in the larger corporate chess blame-game. How can these be better reconciled to get the most out of what technology promises an organisation?

The quickening and changing face of decision-making

Today's business climate does not appear too different from yesteryears. Businesses issue their annual reports more or less in the same format. Leaders still focus on competitive threats and the state of their organisation. Employees still desire job security and personal wellbeing that comes with employment.

Yet look closer and there is an ever-quickening revolution descending upon our business environments. The revolution is driven by the thirst for ever-more accurate and timely information, and the ever-growing list of technologies that promise greater business adaptation and competitive advantage. The impact of this quickening face of decision-making has been coined with several phrases such as 'change is constant' and more recently, 'change fatigue'.

The quickened pace has changed the nature of how decisions are made. Key decisions need to be made on the fly more than ever. Many now occur on email, SMS or a quick video hook-up. Decision channels are more impersonal and increasingly, unprofessional in nature.

I remember reading not long ago how employees in the United States were fired in text messages. Technology now allows access to information anywhere at our fingertips, but it may also cause havoc with our business relationships.

Much of the reason to this accelerated decision-making pace is based on the new role of the consumer. Long gone are those 'image is everything' Andre Agassi tennis commercials from the early 1990s. It was an age driven by product consumerism and brand merchandising. Commercials today choose to pitch community awareness and social inclusiveness. What changed the approach?

For the first time business customers are armed with powerful, consumer-driven technology. Social media platforms and smart phones immediately come to mind. As business customers, we are demanding higher qualitative value from the businesses that serve us. This includes how fast a business responds to what is asked of it. Businesses can no longer just generate profits at the expense of the consumer. The new approach is profit with purpose; maintaining a valued customer experience and greater community relationship. We no longer buy just for the sake of wanting something.

Today the aim of all businesses, both internal to their operations and externally to their customers, is to better obtain and act on higher quality information. Having accurate and timely information is paramount to a business's success. Not only can this information keep existing customers loyal, but it can also discover new customer groups who naturally align to the business.

From an internal business perspective, better qualitative information is not just about year-over-year financial performance numbers. Other business groups such as human resources, marketing and procurement are demanding higher qualitative information for their own decision-making purposes.

The data 'fuel' to produce these higher quality outcomes is primarily found in two places. A company's internal suite of business applications and data it already possesses, and data that exists outside of the company. This external data could come from suppliers, industry associations or perhaps even competitors.

The trick is to combine, or merge, data from these two disparate places to produce higher qualitative information. Who is capable of performing this data merge? One group is the internal information technology (IT) department, and the other group are specialists from technology companies who sell unique products and solutions of their own (with many of these vendors living in the Cloud).

Those businesses that have an IT department will need to rethink the conventional relationship between the IT department and the diverse set of business groups they currently service. Why a rethink?

In the days before consumers had the influence they now do, new technology was pushed out to them from businesses that guessed what they wanted or needed. Before the days of customer experience and social media, consumers really didn't have a voice in the way technology was delivered to them.

This 'push' technology approach meant that IT departments had to be centralised and monolithic to accommodate the big-budget business projects that were sanctioned by the governing boards. With consumers in control of technology outcomes they prefer, businesses are recalibrating their delivery model to be more lightweight and agile so as to better respond to their needs.

In return IT departments are being asked to shift to a 2-speed delivery model. One speed remains slow and monolithic for those big-budget projects that still need to get done. The other speed is delivering business technology agility, new to many IT departments.

With increasing budget cuts placed on many IT departments, how does a department reinvent itself to ensure it can deliver nimbler outcomes with a limited set of resources? There's also the challenge to reorient the delivery mindset for many IT resources. One of my industry colleagues I admire, Rob Livingstone, summed it up best in one of his recent blogs when he wrote:

"Therein lies the challenge for IT departments. If organisations have an ill-defined, outdated or poorly articulated business strategy, then the idea of developing a secure, high value, resilient and adaptive enterprise IT capability is nirvana. It would be like

asking a builder to build the foundation of a building when the architect cannot clearly define the structure and shape of the building (Livingstone 2014)."

So it is not just about changing IT departments. It's also about shifting the strategy and mindset of other business groups from 'telling IT what they need' (read solution thinking), to 'what can my IT shop do for me' (read window shopping for a predisposed service).

To achieve this new business technology relationship requires discussion and commitment at the highest level of the organisation. The quickening pace of decision-making has illustrated the need for structural change from within the organisation. Unlike yesteryear, IT departments should have a vital role to play in this new strategic reorientation. Why are so many technology leaders, like the CIO, not at the executive table then?

Rethinking project delivery governance

From my past experiences as a technology consultant, I've witnessed a range of poor project deliveries. Nearly all suffered from poor planning, and many simply did not have the right stakeholders in the room when they should have.

One often repeated example was that projects were frequently structured to tackle technology solutions as an isolated subset of project delivery. In the early project stages this meant business planning was conducted without the IT team in the room. Business analysts would unknowingly make significant technology assumptions without having their IT department represented. When the business requirements were passed to the IT team, they did not question those assumptions (a mistake onto itself). This led to designing more complex solutions than needed to be. This poor planning coordination would have a knock-on effect when the project started to build and deliver its value.

This typical scenario still happens today. It frankly doesn't make much sense. It's similar to paying a visit to a dentist, telling them what to do with your teeth and showing them the basic procedure on how to do it. The dentist is the tooth expert. We value their judgement and what procedures they perform. Shouldn't those who plan and design technology-based solutions be in the same room when the patient decides they need some technology?

Over time I began to realise these projects forgot the most important engagement principle – the close connection technology has to business value. Tackle one before the other, the project raises the risk that it will miss out on important analysis. Or alternatively it may be incorrect about a range of existing project business assumptions. In a world where technology is embedded everywhere, today it is nearly impossible to perform a business project without adding, altering, removing or affecting some form of technology investment.

I recall a multi-million dollar strategic project to position the organisation to become more competitive through the rollout of new technologies. A business case was prepared and stated 40% of the total project budget would be from introducing new technologies. (Forty percent is considered a high technology investment ratio.)

However, the original business case had many shortcomings. Though it contained detailed expenditures about the technology acquisition, project resources and facility overheads, it failed to identify the highest business delivery risks and assumed no cost variances would exist. It also failed to list critical success factors for the project. Lastly it failed to identify any project dependencies either before or during delivery.

The business case was positioned somewhere between a detailed project management plan and a high-level business case. It tried to accomplish both, but in the process suffered from numerous planning gaps. It wasn't from to lack of skill either. Instead it suffered from a lack of planning quality assurance and governance.

The business case was initially authored between the business unit receiving the investment and the project governance office. The

IT department was only invited to participate once the business case was approved. This meant no technology design expert was invited to provide input to the business case. So therefore no critical design decisions, a key design requirement for ensuring a project's success, were acknowledged or discussed.

With 40% of the budget pertaining to new technology investments, the IT department had no visibility until too late in the design phase. With no proper design discussion, a detailed budget submission lacking contingencies or a clear way of measuring success (other than to implement the technology system), the project suffered a number of significant failures during delivery.

The project took twice as long and more than double the initial forecasts to deliver. It also became a revolving door of project managers, three were shown the door before it was finally delivered. The moral of project members was quite low, and the project gained an unfortunate reputation.

It's no wonder that the low success rate for IT-related projects has not changed from where it was some two decades ago. In fact, some argue that the success percentage has indeed dropped!

In a landmark 1995 study, the Standish Group established that only about 17% of IT projects could be considered "fully successful," another 52% were "challenged" (they didn't meet budget, quality or time goals) and 30% were "impaired or failed." In a recent update of that study conducted for ComputerWorld, Standish examined 3,555 IT projects between 2003 and 2012 that had labor costs of at least $10 million and found that only 6.4% of them were successful (Ditmore 2013).

In many organisations it is still considered best practice to prioritise and deliver projects as the preferred way to spend new capital. However not all business initiatives require formal project structures to achieve their aims. This is especially true in the world of quicker decision making and greater business agility.

Why go through the pain and rigour of a formal project if the change doesn't significantly disrupt a business? If users can continue their roles whilst delivering the change without much role displacement, then shouldn't the initiative be delivered by something other than a traditionally structured project? What about using a ready-made service, or alternatively delivering an agile or lean implementation?

As highlighted in the previous section, this new way of delivering value requires a significant mental shift not only within IT, but also across the various business groups as well. There's of course new processes and structure to also put into place, as well as training of staff.

I would argue adding an agile delivery approach is one of the most challenging issues confronting businesses today. It cannot be done without the CEO's explicit support (and perhaps even the board itself). If it doesn't get top-level support, then there will be a continuation of delivering value the harder way. This will translate to longer delivery cycles, higher costs, higher staff turnover and more management finger pointing and infighting.

In operationalising this dual-delivery approach, the fields of *enterprise architecture* and *change management* have a significant governance assurance role to play. Ensuring that this new agile approach can coexist with conventional project delivery is no easy task to perform. It requires an ability to identify the best approach and then safeguard each approach against the other.

If this is not on your CEO's radar, then here is an invitation to take him or her out for a coffee. Your organisation's IT department, given the proper mandate and skill sets, can play a strategic role in creating your business's digital enterprise. Including the IT department in the earliest stages of planning would free up the organisation's ability to effectively innovate and to discover new competitive advantages. What type of coffee was that?

Three important technology questions everyone should know

If technology is business and business is technology, then business leaders who choose to ignore technology value risk much for their organisation. For leaders who continue to claim technology ignorance, fear not. This section provides a basic crash course on technology value that's guaranteed to pay dividends whilst not 'speaking geek' in the process.

Though not readily apparent, bad technology use can lead to a number of significant organisational problems. These include greater productivity inefficiencies, higher cost of doing business, lower employee retention (for example, too much change in the wrong areas and unrealised business promises), and ingrained silo business governance. Taken together these outcomes over time lead to un-competitiveness and operational stagnation. This is simply from making poor technology decisions.

Implementing technology poorly is just as risky as ignoring the value technology promises. Part of the problem from a management perspective is a decades-old and long-standing perception that IT people are only there to fix things.

I personally love the line from the British comedy show *The IT Crowd*, 'Have you tried turning your computer off and on again?' The show comically demonstrates the perception that IT shops only exist to ensure everything continues to run. The fact that the show's 'IT Crowd' operate out of the company basement is comparable to IT being a utility box; just flick the switch to restore the power.

The perception of being just another critical utility still has some merit. IT of course has a role to play in 'keeping the lights on'. Yet another significant aim of IT shops is to partner with various business units to jointly deliver the best business technology solutions.

As highlighted in the previous section, unfortunately too often there is weak or informal delivery governance tied to this joint solution aim. And therein lies part of the problem.

Unlike the past where all technology was centralised into the IT department, business groups today can ignore the IT department by choosing to take technology they use into the Cloud. They can do so without even notifying their IT department. However, making this independent decision is fraught with risks.

Who will be there to advise them to all the potential traps that come with signing a Cloud service contract, the Cloud vendor? The vendor is unlikely to provide impartial information to the business; they are after all are trying to make a sale with the business in question. Perhaps another business group who has already gone to the Cloud could provide advice? And what happens if the relationship or service goes bad? As the old adage goes 'you don't know what you don't know'.

No IT department should ever be in the position to repair damage that comes from a Cloud decision made without their consent or knowledge. Like any other business group, the IT department must still perform its day job within the organisation and budgets are usually lean.

All of this could simply be avoided by a C-level engagement principle akin to, 'first seek to engage IT on any technology planning manner before engaging technology vendors'. Shouldn't it be the goal of every business leader to prevent bad technology decisions to the best of their organisation's ability?

Returning again to the question, 'how much should business leaders know about technology?' Simply deferring any technology matter to someone else no longer applies. In today's climate of 'technology is business and business is technology', that action is just too risky.

When I would meet a key business leader for the first time, I would pitch my value like this: 'I work as a technology planner in this organisation and kindly ask for your permission to not invest in technology unless you know its value before I do.' I found this statement usually grabbed their attention, especially as it came from a person who was in a technology role. It was not something they expecting to hear.

I cannot emphasize this point enough – please don't waste money on something unless the technology intent is clearly understood. Here are three simple questions any leader can use to help tease out technology intent:

a) Is technology delivering **'value-add'** to my current operational model?

b) Is technology expected to help me **transform** my existing operational model?

c) Is technology being asked **to do both**?

If the answers are known, then all is clear and good. If the answers are unknown, then any planning should be immediately put on hold until everyone agrees to the purpose of the technology under consideration.

Why is this so important? The business delivery risks for each of these questions are notably different. Not knowing the answer can cost much more time and money than originally anticipated. Using these simple questions as a tool will save organisations from many unnecessary technology upgrades and 'special interest projects'.

The questions are designed to do more than enquire about the technology value proposition. They implicitly ask business related things. If the technology answer is unknown, there is probably a deeper business unknown at work here. It could be lack of clarity to a business's operation model, or perhaps a set of business requirements that are too technical in nature. In either case technology-related projects should not proceed until there is a sharp and clear business imperative so that the technology value can be properly linked to these imperatives.

The first two questions also align to the organisational planning coin introduced in the earlier section, 'Strategy in today's operating climate'. The following illustration shows the intersection between the two.

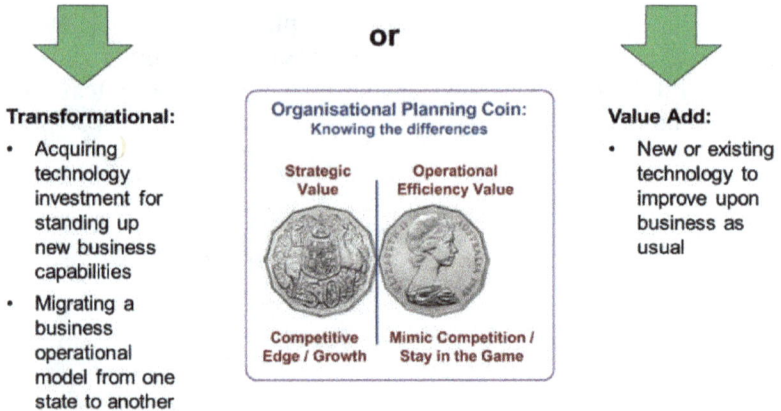

Transformational:

- Acquiring technology investment for standing up new business capabilities
- Migrating a business operational model from one state to another

Organisational Planning Coin:
Knowing the differences

Strategic Value | Operational Efficiency Value

Competitive Edge / Growth | Mimic Competition / Stay in the Game

Value Add:

- New or existing technology to improve upon business as usual

Armed with the three questions, the answers can be plotted against the annual capital planning process to determine how many technology-based initiatives are about tweaking the operational model, and how many are for transforming the business. A quick count could easily determine how technology value is being delivered in their organisation.

For example, if most of the technology investments are being spent on operational efficiencies then technology delivery is not seen as a business strategic tool. The same is true in reverse. The business-technology risk profile will thereby be different. Knowing how technology is delivered is a great barometer of that organisation's competitive maturity. After all, technology is business and business is technology.

The consumer now reigns supreme – please bow

Consumer choice, or the choice people make in deciding who to do business with, has replaced decades of consumer materialism. It's a world where consumers demand and seek out higher quality value for the goods and services they purchase. They are no longer wedded to a particular brand or trendy product. As a society we are flocking to online channels, like social media, to arm us with better information in making wiser choices. With the online power to name and shame, consumers are also less likely to tolerate service they find unacceptable.

To underscore the accelerated pace of this consumer change, Deloitte recently issued a report that found a whopping 53% of Australians now have on average three electronic devices – a laptop, smart phone and tablet (Timson 2014). That's over half of the population connected to the digital environment wherever they are!

What are Aussies doing with these devices? Watching less and less television in their lounge room as the preferred mode for entertainment and news. The report forecasts that in the next 12 months, "people who will stick with watching physical media (TV, DVDs, discs) most or all the time will drop to 42 per cent (Timson 2014)." And how does Australia compare to other countries? "The report found Australia has more "digital omnivores", at 53 per cent, than the US (37 per cent) and Japan (17 per cent), but fewer than Norway and China (Timson 2014)."

Let me share my own example of this new customer-driven world. Some seven years ago I was a senior manager for a large intercity transportation organisation. When I joined, the organisation had an existing mentality driven by 'safety first'. This included a view that fleet management (which included passenger safety) was one of the most important business drivers, and rightfully so. The view originated from several headline-grabbing accidents that badly tainted the organisation some years earlier.

Generally speaking, the commuter timetable (or when trains arrive at their destination) was considered a secondary priority to fleet management. This view was reasonable as long as there was enough timetable slack in the system to ensure customer satisfaction levels remained high.

However as waves of commuters began using the fleet network as a cheaper and safer form of transportation, the existing timetable began to show significant inefficiencies. People began to voice dissatisfaction through various social media channels including twitter (which was a fairly new social media channel at that time). Mainstream news agencies also began printing negative online feeds and tweets, adding fuel to the fire.

Other commuters, who were generally less vocal in the traditional sense, now joined the bandwagon as well to voice their frustrations. It became a negative feedback loop. I clearly remember near-daily negative media stories about the organisation I had just joined. Something had to give.

A new CEO was appointed and immediately set about changing the priority of the organisation to make commuter satisfaction the top priority. Like any large and mature business, many initially resisted the change in direction. I particularly remember one colleague I spoke with who said 'why should we bother? The commuters will just have to accept the timetable as it is.'

Little by little, the organisation did in fact make significant traction. It eventually rolled out a new timetable that was preferential to the commuter, not the fleet management system. There were a series of customer-oriented education programs for frontline staff, and it dedicated more public relation resources to cover positive stories of improvements the organisation was making.

Two short years on, the public perception had completely turned around. It was an organisation that was meeting the demands of the public it served. The organisation I worked for was indeed making major strides in becoming a customer-friendly business.

The consumer now reigns supreme. It's a world where customer retention and loyalty sit at the top of the business pyramid. Consumers make regular use of 'likes and dislikes', star ratings and post commentary about their experiences. If a customer has a positive experience they are more likely to recommend it to others. The facts are quite telling. Here are two notable stats extracted from a 2014 Vision customer survey by Optus SingTel:

- *Of those customers who reacted to a bad experience, nearly half told a friend, family member or colleague, **23 percent** researched or considered a competitor and another **10 percent** actually left;*

- ***27% to 41%** - the percentage of surveyed customers who expect a personalised, flexible experience is set to grow significantly over the next 1–2 years;*

Technology is the consumer fuel and has become entrenched in our everyday lives. Most of us now live and breathe with a smart phone or tablet by our side. Instantaneous information at our fingertips anytime, anywhere enabling real-time decisions is now the norm.

The digital age has well and truly arrived. The technology frontiers continue to be pushed to find ever-greater digital benefits. Consumers can now create useable items with 3-d printing. They can purchase robots to perform elementary tasks in the home or Google Glasses to receive information directly into their lenses. Digital inventions have exploded onto our consumer radar.

At its core the digital age is the convergence of three things, technology, information and the consumer. Each component feeds off the other, accelerating the pace of change and in return, heightening the consumer demand for business results. There's a quickening pace of business change and here's one way to view this cycle.

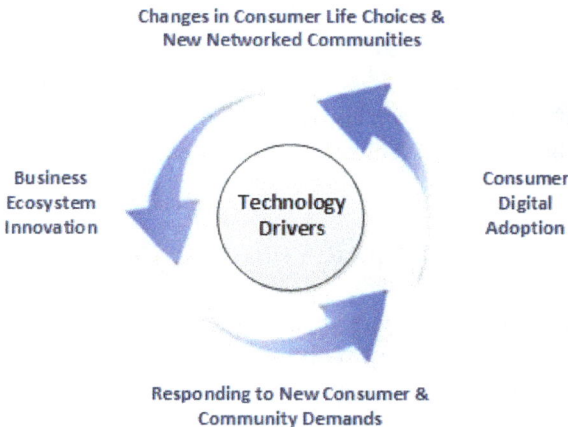

Changes in Consumer Life Choices &
New Networked Communities

Business
Ecosystem
Innovation

Technology
Drivers

Consumer
Digital
Adoption

Responding to New Consumer &
Community Demands

Borrowing from the character Jerry Maguire, consumers are demanding 'show me the information' when considering purchases. If that wasn't enough, consumers are increasingly discovering and passing judgment about a business and its competitors like never before.

The key question for businesses today is not *if* they should invest in consumer-driven technology, but *how* fast and where. Understanding what the *consumer wants* is central to everything the business does. It's about thinking how a mobile app can perform certain types of transactions customers want to perform *and* how the app also generates benefits for the business.

It's about building benefits for both the customer and the organisation. Doing so will gain more customers and also reinforce loyalty with existing customers. It's asking questions such as, 'how does my business, through new technology innovations, make it easier for our customers to do business with us?'

This new mindset is changing the nature of business decisions. Customer satisfaction reports are featuring in boardroom discussions and now sit equal to more traditional reporting based on higher business performance and efficiencies.

In turn, this new mindset is forcing some fundamental changes within the business corridors of influence. The roles of marketing and technology departments have been thrust into the executive limelight and onto customer-driven strategic plans. A new mindset opens the doors to a new approach in performing strategic management. It's an approach grounded in greater understanding of the consumer and the use of technology.

Information as a tradable commodity

Over the past few years it is difficult to read mainstream newspapers or surf the Internet without coming across references such as 'explosion of data', the value of 'big data', debates about what is 'metadata', and my favourite tagline, 'data as a currency'. It's as if the world has once again focused its collective energy on that once nefarious 'information age' tagline from the late 1990s.

What is quite different this time around is the sheer amount of data our society is recording and consuming. The stats are simply mind-blowing about the collective size of our digitised data.

Google has estimated if you tried to calculate the amount of information captured from the dawn of civilisation until 2003, it would equal about 5 exabytes of data (or 1 billion billions, a number with 18 zeros behind it!). A decade later in 2013 the world was producing this same amount of information every 2 days (GilPress 2013). Truly mind bending stuff. Has the world finally reached some sort of tipping point to harness information (defined as useful, meaningful data) as a tradable commodity?

Consumers expect that any digital service they sign-up for will allow them access to a rich set of information. And consumers are right to expect this.

To illustrate an example a customer can telephone their insurance company and expect to retrieve information about their policy details, their payment history, and any claims that have been processed. They would also expect to see the same thing using the insurance provider's online service.

If the customer is thinking of switching insurance policies, they may decide to look at another site that compares competitor products, rather than choosing to read a printed product brochure from the mail. The decision to select another competing policy will most likely be based on criteria from the comparison website.

As explored earlier, the quickened pace of decision making is forcing businesses to examine the latency of information. In the above example, a product brochure has to arrive in the mailbox at the time someone might be contemplating reviewing or switching policies. Otherwise, it has no tangible information value. Any other time it arrives it'll probably disappear into the bin.

To reduce this information latency requires getting the timing right. Getting the timing right is again better knowing your customers. Why print thousands of brochures using a traditional scattergun marketing campaign when a business can instead examine their customer data to better target customers to send the brochure to?

Speaking of mailing brochures, in many parts of the world government post offices have seen significant decline in letter volumes. Consumers and businesses alike are making the switch to online services, such as opting for electronic bills and invoices, as opposed to printed ones sent through the mail. As a result, post office employment numbers have tumbled in recent years. Paradoxically there is an increased consumer need for more personalised parcel delivery services – a perfect opportunity for postal organisations to diversify their operations to cater for this consumer trend.

With businesses continuing to collect more and more customer information, the ability to exchange information between businesses is also steadily increasing. Many now collect secondary data about their customers. Secondary data does not provide direct value to the business, but it might provide direct value to other businesses that may be interested in acquiring it.

Think of a fictional large retail bank for a moment. This financial institution not only collects core-banking transactions, it also collects demographic details about their diverse customers.

Like many of its competitors, the bank helps to sponsor several charitable campaigns throughout the year. It does this by offering to collect donations from its banking members and transfer these to the appropriate charity.

One of the charities recognises an opportunity to closer partner with the bank. If it knew who had donated and where they were located, it would significantly reduce their expenses for marketing and public relations activities. It could also increase their charity's profile and membership numbers in targeting like-minded individuals. The bank, in turn, benefits in not only increased goodwill, it could reinforce this goodwill through offering customer loyalty points or other incentives recognising those who contributed.

The example details the powerful use of swapping specific customer information. Obviously privacy laws allow consumers to opt out of their details being sent to other organisations.

However, this does not preclude an organisation from aggregating multiple data records into a single, summarised data view of a particular business area. This summarised data view is one form of data analytics, one of the hottest fields within businesses at the moment.

An aggregated set of data does not include personal details of John Smith who lives at Somewhere Place, Nowhereville. The sharing of this data does not violate the privacy laws and is indeed transferable to marketing or advertising firms keen to gain better knowledge about buying trends and generic consumer online behaviour.

It is a great business leap to put a market price on this information and throw it into a tradable market where organisations bid on its value. To create a tradable market, a few conditions must first exist.

First there has to be an agreeable level of data standards so that it can be fairly distributed and traded. For many years this had been a significant hurdle. Industry persistence over the past several decades has now ensured both technical and business-level standards exist for how data is exchanged.

Data also requires a common repository, a clearinghouse if you will, so that it can be quickly moved in and out of a market. This is where a technology platform is required to perform the clearinghouse role. And similar to how data is now exchanged, these platforms have existed for some time.

So the pre-requisites required to build and operate a tradable information market are already in place. Many businesses have already started to create private markets to operate their 'information trading platform'.

A private market is where transactions are limited between two or more known parties and are bound to the form all the parties agree to up front. The size of the private market can vary. One example where this is already happening is in oil and gas where different businesses are trading geometric information.

Another example of tradable platforms is in the software industry where for a significant user fee, a business can acquire an external data set. Many of these data sets are based on geometric location data.

Society is inching closer to the age of 'data as a currency'. It has already accepted the novel and new currency channel, bitcoins. When the world begins trading information in public markets, it may again enter a new competitive era. This business leap is perhaps not such a big leap after all.

Turning data into currency translates to new revenue streams for businesses of many types. Is your organisation thinking about the monetisation of its data? What it might mean to how your business is structured and governed? Have you considered a Chief Data Officer role, or alternatively a senior Information Architect for your strategy and planning group?

Technology now spearheading innovation

The continuing rise of technology's role in society is redefining, or perhaps recasting, the value of business. Technology is accelerating the pace of business innovation like never before. Technology's earlier role in better, more efficient automated business processes or in more exciting, feature-rich products was the business battleground in gaining a competitive edge, but this is much less so now.

In my conversations with senior leaders, many believe technology no longer simply enables the organisation to operate better. Instead it has become a driving force to creating strategic opportunities outside the traditional business boundaries. To put it another way, technology innovation today is a lever for instituting significant business change.

In a rare and symbolic move the Reserve Bank of Australia (RBA), Australia's central bank, said in June 2014 that Australian companies must innovate in this digital disruption or else become extinct. The RBA official, Sarv Girn who was speaking at an economic conference of business leaders, was quoted as saying:

> *"We now see wearable technology and 3D printing knocking on the door to introduce another wave of change in health, manufacturing and no doubt many other industry sectors… the biggest risk of all is to not do anything at all – ignoring the waves of digital disruption in business and society has led to extinction for many (Greber 2014)."*

The fact that the RBA, a federal finance institution, discussed the importance of technology innovation to the financial health of businesses is a significant sign of the times. It's symbolic as it represents the close relationship between the financial and technology markets.

It's once again the consumer that is fuelling this technology innovation like never before. The result is a reshaping of the consumer-to-business landscape. Products and gadgets alone are out, replaced by customer loyalty and social value. Not only is the competitive landscape being redefined, technology innovation is also drawing into question existing internal business structures.

Traditional business boundaries are largely founded on command and control management structures; those vertical decision-making hierarchies where decisions flow up, not across. These structures are coming under increasing stress as new technology 'areas of interest' force more cross-functional business activities.

What are these? We read about them nearly every day. They are the terms labelled as business agility, digital, data analytics, information security, customer experiences and procurement to name a few. Each one of these is not confined to a traditional command and control business silo.

However, there is a major obstacle. Achieving cross-functional business value in the land of command and control can only be achieved through greater awareness, collaboration and living a set of ascribed organisational values. Delivering upon these requires a re-evaluation of management styles and approaches to leadership.

Turning to leadership, one effect of this internal disruption is the number and diversity of new C-level management roles being created. The traditional Chief Information Officer (CIO) now must compete with newly minted roles such as Chief Technology Officer, Chief Digital Officer, Chief Information Security Officer, Chief Customer Officer and the Chief Business Technology Officer. I cannot remember a time where there has been more talk and experimentation of new C-level roles during my quarter century as an able-bodied worker.

Adding more confusion, each one of these roles is defined quite differently in each organisation. How to make sense of this madness? There is no clear-cut set of instructions for the creation C-level roles. It is a highly disruptive business environment trying to make sense of this new consumer-led technology frontier.

This C-level role confusion signals two truisms. One confirms a massive digital transformation is well underway, of which some businesses are further into their consumer transformation journey than others.

The second truism is the war for talent continues to intensify. Finding talented people who can fill these C-level roles, and help guide the organisation in making that transition successful, will be a challenge in the years to come. In a cheekily written article for Forbes entitled *"Don't let a Chief Digital Officer steal the best part of your job"*, Dan Woods articulates this war on talent when he writes:

Attention CIOs and CTOs, the best part of your job is under attack. If you don't get ahead of the trend toward the Chief Digital

Officer role, your job may become a technology backwater, which is never what you had in mind. Many CIOs and CTOs have never fought hard enough to assert themselves as business executives. Instead, most have laid a strong claim to technology expertise. Nobody thinks of a CDO as a geek. Rather, a CDO is supposed to be a Steve Jobs wannabe, someone who sees all the technology and business pieces on the table and puts together a transformational new product, service, or way of working (Woods 2014).

All of these C-level adaptations and permutations are not isolated to the inner management circle. Examining the evolving role of the IT architect (or technology design guru) is a fascinating way to learn how technology is becoming ever more important within an organisation.

Just a few decades ago an IT architect was a technology specialist who could better illustrate complex, physical environments. These included things like networking diagrams, programming frameworks and relational database design, truly the black box stuff non-technical people don't care to know about.

The next generation architect started to connect those physical environments together to provide real world business solutions. These architects are still working today in large, complex project environments. Their value is immense as they can keep implementation costs down and design a solution that stands the test of time.

About a decade ago a more generalist 'Enterprise Architect', or EA, role emerged. Its purpose is to provide holistic value across the organisation. It is a role meant to position technology decisions as being more strategic and less project centric. Today's EAs tackle strategic approaches to Cloud providers, mobile devices, security concerns, organisation-wide data challenges, and the standardisation of technology products and technology development practices just to name a few.

As this role requires both broad technology and business knowledge, it is considered a senior-level organisational planning role.

The EA no longer needs to not come from a technology background as their core skill.

This is yet another 'war on talent' example, finding top talent to deliver top-level strategic management. No longer is strategic talent only sourced from the financial end of town. Architects who understand businesses strategy and speak in business language are fast filling vital strategic roles.

It is not just about IT architects either. There are a number of new mid-level management roles that have emerged to include Agile Coaches, Scrum Masters, Change Managers and Cloud Brokers.

They all have a common thread; each role delivers cross-functional value. These roles are new attempts at finding better ways of engaging between various business groups. The same business groups who all desire greater say and involvement in those technology investment decisions. The same business groups who are also being asked to provide better and more innovative technology value to their customers.

It all makes for very interesting and testing times.

PART C:

Today's Approaches & Challenges

CHAPTER 6:

Selling Strategy Within the Business

"*Measurement is the first step that leads to control and eventually to improvement. If you can't measure something, you can't understand it. If you can't understand it, you can't control it. If you can't control it, you can't improve it.*"

– H. James Harrington

The quote came from a best-selling book entitled, *Business Process Improvement*. The book was written in the early 1990s when operational efficiencies were the centre of everyone's dartboard. I believe the time has come to apply this quote to the other side of the planning coin, strategic growth. If I apply Harrington's concept to this side of the coin, it might sound something like this:

- *Why commit to a significant organisational trade-off if you don't fully understand it?*

- *If you don't fully understand the trade-off, then how could you plan to deliver it?*

- *If you can't plan to deliver it, then how do you measure its success?*

Nearly every time I attend an event or listen to a presentation, I now hear the words 'evidence-based'. Measuring things to better understand them is the essence of providing sound evidence. Sound evidence ensures better outcomes, at any level. Recognising the value of this approach is no longer good enough. Far more important is making this approach part of the furniture, or one's management tools of trade. This is the key challenge.

This chapter describes various approaches to performing strategic management. Each of these approaches offers a way to measuring intended business value.

I often say if you can't, or choose not to measure something, then don't bother discussing it. This may sound a bit brash and direct, but in certain situations it is needed. Situations where there are too many 'fluffy' discussions, or meetings that are aimless and lacking purpose. Talk is cheap; action is what counts and evidence is the engine room.

Conflict negotiation no longer applies

"Feedback in conflict is a gift (Freeman 2014)." I love this statement from the renowned business philosopher Ed Freeman. He was speaking at a conference I attended last year when I heard these words. The statement was in reference to the importance of collecting feedback when conflict is at its highest, a moment where feedback can spark the greatest of innovations.

I believe this principle can be applied to strategic management. Strategy is ultimately about making touch choices, or trade-offs. A situation where there is always some tension and potential for conflict. Preparing for this situation is the key. Good planning can capture this conflict and harness it as an opportunity to initiate a change. The alternative to a trade-off is compromise, and this can be the death of any innovative approach.

My personal interest in conflict (and negotiation) dates back to my earliest days in high school where I participated in several Model United Nation (MUN) conferences. My team and I would, to the best of our abilities, represent a pre-selected country to tackle the hot political issues of the day. I remember one such occasion in the mid-1980s attending the Den Hague Model UN conference.

Our team represented the African country of Burkina Faso. Upon learning we had been given a country that was one of the poorest in the world, our hearts sank because we didn't get a larger country that had prestige and influence.

That feeling didn't last long. At the time the country had just changed their official name from Upper Volta to Burkina Faso. None of the conference attendees had the slightest idea who we were. We turned this confusion into an asset.

We were able to argue from any position we wanted. We didn't have the shackles of representing a country like Germany or China where everyone already knew their positions on most issues. The freedom to choose any position meant others vied for our vote on many issues in the General Assembly. We turned what first appeared to be a negative into an opportunity to be creative.

It was during the many MUN conferences I attended I came to learn it is best to argue down to a position worth ultimately seeking. It is the case of presenting the initial position as a bit more radical so that the eventual compromise can ensue. Obviously this is not new concept, but for the teenager I was, it was a great lesson in life.

I carried my interest for conflict resolution into my university studies where I gained more insights on the human side of the negotiation process. One of those elements is the intensity of the pre-negotiation process. Participants wrangle over seating arrangements, what belongs on the table, 'who sits where', and the rules of engagement. It may achieve the right negotiation platform environment, but it does not buy success during the negotiation.

As so much time is spent on the pre-negotiation process there is usually little time left for the negotiation itself. It is no wonder that publically-hosted negotiations rarely get deals across. There is just too much pressure on all sides to not capitulate on their demands (in the eyes of each other) and too little time in which to meaningfully discuss things.

Negotiations are best done either behind closed doors or through third party intermediaries. A classic example is the famous deal struck between the PLO and Israel using Norway as a back-channel negotiation platform. At the time no one knew this was happening as the world's attention was focused on the public negotiations at the Madrid conference.

Why does any of this matter to strategic management? The process of negotiation and compromise was the order of the day in the Kaizen-influenced business world. The preferred approach was through governance mechanisms that encouraged the art of negotiation and compromise such as capital planning processes. In a command and control business structure that encouraged business silos, new efficiencies could be discussed and then prioritising according to 'who argued best'.

This approach, noble as it may seem, leads to nothing more than an agreed number of operational improvements. Tweak that system over there, adjust this business process here, or initiate a new HR policy for that group there. Ideas about doing something radically different have been removed from the group discussion. Being naturally risk-adverse, management accepts the lowest common denominator as the approved list of things to do.

The end result is similar to a collection of rock stars performing on stage but who keep fine-tuning their instruments in mid-song. Their music gets frequently interrupted for more fine-tuning. Fans are beginning to boo the band for their repeated musical interruptions. Each member of the band has missed the point as to why they are on stage, to perform as one group in creating harmonious music. Somehow they thought it easier to fine-tune their instruments during their live act than to perform a band dress rehearsal.

I stopped counting the number of times managers forget why they are on stage to perform. Their KPIs keep telling them to fine-tune their instruments. So they do.

Tough trade-offs that are core to any strategic plan are in fact, negotiated away. What remains is what management always wanted, something each felt they could manage, as opposed to something that, in their eyes, would not be worth the effort to do before the actual performance.

Here is the most important point. These managers lived in a world of operational efficiencies and were following the logical and correct path. It was easier to demonstrate a case for making an operational tweak than to agree to a new organisational direction. To reinforce this thinking, H. James Harrington and others gave direction to achieving operational improvements through an evidence-based approach.

This is akin to the concept of a self-fulfilling prophecy. Senior management did not support the strategic direction because they believed it was not achievable from a lack of sound evidence. Without a full commitment and belief in a strategic plan, managers will revert back to their silo operational concerns.

In fact, many operational managers today are still glued to this thinking. It is grounded on decades of employment experience of knowing what works. Many organisations continue to support antiquated hierarchical management structures and corporate governance mechanisms. In the earlier part of the book I termed this as an APE (Application of Process Efficient) planning environment. I believe this old way of operating is the defining challenge for these businesses.

Yet in today's new consumer-oriented business landscape, this conflict resolution approach to performing strategic management simply does not apply. Once a new direction is set, managers need to support that direction and encourage others to rally behind them. Strategists have an important role to play in building that evidence-based case to mitigate managers concerns and ensure they have confidence in the path forward.

No more stupid strategic execution

So your business has a vision and direction in mind and is ready to initiate significant change. How do you get started down the execution path? Who do you bring to the table? What skills must people possess? How involved should your operations team? The list of questions can seem endless.

As highlighted earlier in the book, the art of strategy execution is by far the most challenging. A 2010 McKinsey Global Survey concluded that implementing strategy is one of the biggest frustrations amongst executives. For those organisations in the survey *not* labelled as 'effective developers of strategy', just 22% believed their strategic management processes were fully embedded into their capital planning set of processes (Birshan, Dye and Hall 2011).

Perhaps addressing the context, approach and structures to strategy execution could be an initial step. Like most things in life, it is to best to first understand the organisational landscape, or environment, before charging ahead with an effective approach. The contextual organisational landscape can be thought of as the current state of the organisation.

One way to determine the business readiness state is to think about how stable your organisation is. For example, here are some qualifying questions to consider with no particular priority or weighting:

- ***Ownership question:*** *Do your shareholders / equity partners and your board accept major business transformation is required?*

- ***Leadership question:*** *Does your organisation have a stable executive leadership team? (No recent leadership spills or adversarial relationships exist.)*

- **_Staff question:_** _Have all major transformation initiatives finished or wound down? (To avoid the possibility of change fatigue.)_

If you answered 'yes' to all three questions, your organisation may be well placed to undertake major organisational change. All involved stakeholders are aligned to create a well-positioned business climate.

If you answered 'no' to one or more of the above, you may want to consider how you would re-position those affected groups for a pending change. You may also wish to consider any scenarios that have a high risk of derailing a change program.

Another contextual consideration is the reason to change the organisation. It is the, 'why are we doing this?' There are many modelling techniques in the market to assess this question. Here are three simple ways to classify the type of change:

1. **_External Threat_** _– examples include new competitive entrants to existing market, or poor brand or business identity causing market confusion._

2. **_Inward Pressure*_** _– examples include poor quality of its good and services, management spill or restructure, and mergers._

3. **_Opportunistic_** _– examples include an acquisition, and innovation programs to capture un-tapped markets or leapfrog competition._

* Exclusions include like-for-like management replacement, reining in costs or adopting tighter fiscal management controls, as these examples tend to fall into more of an operational efficiency planning cycle.

The first two classifications, External Threat & Inward Pressure, require a necessity to act upon a business imperative. The third is not considered a necessity but rather a proactive type of change.

There may be more than just one reason triggering an organisation to instigate change. Segmenting a strategic execution program to each of these reasons can help keep communications simple and messaging clear. A cautionary note here. Adding a second or third type of change to the mix will add significant complexity. As the old adage goes, it is better to do a few things well than to do many things poorly.

Knowing the current state of readiness and the 'why' should not become a drawn out, time sapping, vetting process. After all, the targeted vision awaits its set of instructions. The current state is indeed necessary but shouldn't be a deal breaker or reason to postpone change.

Once the right context is painted, it is time to think about the *approach and delivery structure* for an execution strategy.

Yesteryear's approach to performing strategic change meant that strategy implementation followed strategy planning. That is not necessarily the case today.

Large transformation programs are still performed but the process is no longer monolithic. Many programs are carved out into smaller planning and implementation stages. Some stages are also run in parallel 'planning and delivery streams' to make them more business agile and responsive.

There are various execution structures to also consider. Does your execution strategy include a set of formal structured projects, a leaner delivery style, or perhaps a set of piloted programs? Pilots that can test the change resolve of a particular part of the organisation before committing to deliver wider change to the organisation. Maybe it's a hybrid of all three structures?

Each of these approaches and structures has their merits and corresponding delivery risks. Finding the right recipe should be the job of the chief strategist or senior strategy team.

There is still something missing; having greater clarity around who, what, where, why and how. It's essentially about *setting internal organisational expectations*.

This is incredibly important and often missed initial step. We all have an innate need to understand what the organisation is planning to do, why and where it is doing it, who will it affect and how.

Distributing a before and after organisation chart is simply not enough to ease people's minds. Doing so will only communicate the message of a management restructure without creating understanding of the purpose (other than the assumed cost cutting). If the organisation is to move in a new direction, then ensuring everyone is on the same page is perhaps the single most important planning step to perform.

What if there was a single way to represent each and every organisation on the planet. This includes the biggest global banks to the smallest of small entrepreneurial businesses. Such a model could be used to pinpoint or highlight areas change was occurring. It could provide a baseline in initiating strategic discussion from anywhere in the organisation. It wouldn't matter if someone worked in finance, marketing or sales, their expectations could be easily explained and aligned from one unifying diagram.

Management

Who sits where

The OrgPi Model

People
Capital
Brand

Capabilities

What the
organisation does

ORGANISATION

Goods & Services

How and when
value is delivered

This model represents three pillars of strategic execution, a) the management team which is responsible for the decision-making effectiveness, b) the goods and services the organisation ultimately provides, and c) its capabilities that allow those good and services to be produced. All three rely on each other for support. Tweaking one end-point has thereby an effect on the other two. In the centre of the model are the core elements to every organisation – people, capital and brand (or its identity). Each of these core elements not only influences the end-points but also the relationships between the end-points.

The diagram can be applied in multiple ways. In the next section I describe an example of one such way.

The last thing to consider is a *good-fit framework* for the execution plan. A framework is nothing more than an orderly classification of a set of ideas and principles that is used to help guide business best practices. Frameworks are good at providing business guidance. They perform this by providing a way to rationalise an important set of decisions. Models and diagrams most always underpin frameworks.

There are many frameworks that cover the field of strategic management. Most are industry specific, like SOSTAC for strategic digital marketing, TOGAF for enterprise architecture, and PROSCI for change management to name a few.

A framework can add value in two ways. First it can guide the planning process for the strategic execution plan. Secondly and perhaps most important, keep all on board who are not familiar with strategic management practices, ensuring they feel comfortable about how things are progressing.

Similarly, I find a framework can counter any naysayers and doomsayers who would otherwise seek to challenge the program's validity. Not having key constituents understand (or those who wish to challenge) strategic management practices is perhaps the single, biggest risk to implementing a strategic plan for an organisation.

In my line of work as a technology and business strategist I choose to not reference a framework to my audience. Doing so is too much detail, an un-necessary overhead to potentially causing greater confusion. Instead I adopt the framework into my own mental modal, using its rationale for the discussion at hand. It need not be explicitly expressed.

Here's a final tip. When thinking about the skills necessary to perform strategic management, it's essential during the interview to ask a candidate to describe a framework they have used, and how they used it to better rationalise a critical business decision. I have found these few questions usually weed out the pretenders from the contenders. Candidates also need to model well as we'll explore in the next section.

Business modelling – the great organisation unifier

I often say if a picture tells a thousand words, then an effective diagram can tell ten thousand words. If the purpose is to communicate a complex situation, then breaking it down into a visual diagram can simplify communication and reduce time to digest vital information (as opposed to reading it in a wordy document).

Most decision makers don't need to understand all the details of the diagram. They simply want assurance that the diagram can effectively communicate the key messages they need to convey to their audiences.

A good diagram is similar to a well-constructed house blueprint. If an architect arrived with various blueprint options, highlighting in easy-to-understand terms the differences between the options, the homeowner would think 'this is someone I can do business with'. The architect is letting the blueprint speak for itself. He or she does not need to explain things beyond the diagram because this might complicate the discussion and therefore devalue that experience with them. This is primarily why architects put so much value on those blueprints.

I have often thought about why we are so compelled to believe a well-formed diagram, model or blueprint. I believe they act as a bridge between the creative and analytical worlds, or our left and right brains.

If someone is analytical and another thinks creatively, it can be a challenge to effectively communicate complex situations. Take a situation where a creative person is visualising something in their head yet struggles to put into words this image for an analytical-thinking person.

As the analytical person listens he or she responds by deciphering the words into a linear, step-by-step interpretation. The creative person then struggles to appreciate how this interpretation fits into a larger context. Each gets frustrated with the other as each is failing to understand the relevance to the other's approach and thinking.

A well-formed diagram can communicate to both sides in a way that words and steps simply cannot.

What continues to disturb me is how often management make critical, strategic decisions using either a document containing only words, or by a string of financial numbers and tables. In an ever-more complex world we live in shouldn't we look to rationalise our mutual expectations into models and diagrams? These images expose us to important insights and objectivity that may go missed in endorsing decisions.

Here's a test. If I were a leader making a decision on a sizeable investment I know will alter a significant part of my company, would I simply trust words and numbers?

Yes, a rational argument can indeed be made from words and from sound financial numbers to support it. However, if leaders and managers cannot visualise a target state to how the business is going to be remodelled, then there is no business roadmap. Without a high-level roadmap to guide decisions, the business may be able to deliver the strategic aims but will likely spend double the effort, capital and time to get there.

In this scenario the strategic decision comes first, then an execution plan is later crafted to figure out the 'how'. As explored in the previous section this was the older, preferred way to perform strategy execution. It is a high-risk, disconnected strategic management approach that no longer works for this new business age.

Here is a simple example to how models can be used within a business roadmap context. I'll choose to use the OrgPi model illustrated in the previous section as a basis. The below diagram articulates how a three-year transformation program can be contextually represented.

Company A: 3-year Business Roadmap

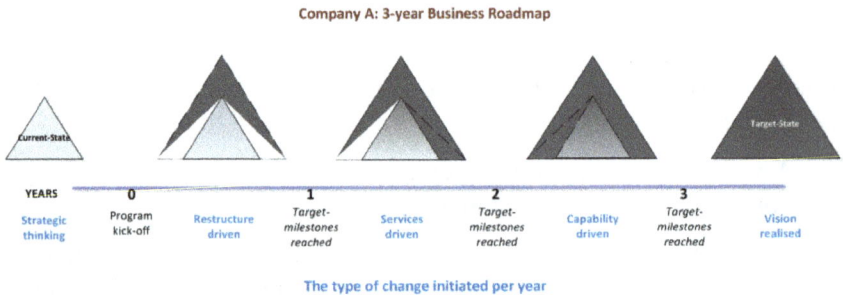

YEARS	0		1		2		3	
Strategic thinking	Program kick-off	Restructure driven	Target-milestones reached	Services driven	Target-milestones reached	Capability driven	Target-milestones reached	Vision realised

The type of change initiated per year

Imagine this situation, the executive team recognises that its organisation cannot perform a management restructure, service realignment, and operational model (or capabilities) change all at once. The organisation simply would not survive the accumulative wave of changes placed upon it. The resulting impact would most likely send the organisation many years backwards from its intended 3-year vision. Instead, the change is divided into three major phases to lessen the transition burden within the organisation.

The organisation's primary aim is to retain its valuable customers during the transformation so it has chosen to first restructure its management hierarchy to better preserve the state of the business during the subsequent stages of transformation. This includes a program to retain its existing employees to ensure they remain happy and passionate about the business during a period of significant change.

Management has decided to schedule the services-driven change between years one and two instead of the final stage to quicken new business growth. This assumes that existing staff can be trained to provide support to these new revenue streams. The organisation has set a target of 50% increase in revenue at the end of its 3-year transformation.

This is why changes to its capabilities should be performed in the last stage. The revenue target is simply speculative at this early planning phase. Halfway through the transformation the organisation will have a better appreciation of whether it can meet its target. To prevent a potential cost of sale blowout, the organisation should not invest in new assets and people (capabilities) until it can better understand where it is in its journey.

This simple change diagram can be a powerful communication tool within the organisation. It's a contextual validation of the narrative. If needed, more layers can be added to the diagram to make it a more engaging communication tool.

A shared understanding of where the organisation is headed is absolutely essential to its success. A few hours spent crafting a diagram together, with management consent, could help to save significant dollars in the retention of good talent. That is the power of modelling at work!

CEO's 7 lucky numbers to measuring value

If strategic management is part research and forecasting, then it stands to reason that measuring those promised values is absolutely critical. Otherwise, why perform strategic management. Measuring the effectiveness of the effort is essential to ensure the execution remains on track for a successful delivery.

What type of things should be measured? A good place to start is to ask a CEO or Managing Director what keeps them up at night. I found it could be put down to 7 basic items of most concern to their business. The following table describes these '7 lucky numbers' along with some ways on how they may be measured.

#	Business Measurement Type	Function Most Aligned to	Example Ways to Measure
1	Increase Revenue	Sales	Attract more clients or secure additional funding
2	Increase Workforce / Production Efficiencies	Operational – Support	Lower costs, increase qualitative outputs
3	Improve Decision-Making Capabilities	Operational - Management	Better use / collection of information
4	Supplemental Transformative Growth	Strategy / Planning	Program success with business change initiatives
5	Elevate Brand Awareness / PR	Marketing	Targeted campaigns and events
6	Augment Compliance & Policy Enforcement	Legal / Quality & Risk Assurance	Testing the effectiveness of hard governance structures
7	Raise Human Capital Value	Human Resources	Increase staff retention and alignment of company values

These lucky 7 are a way to measure organisational progress, an overarching framework meant to classify how value can be measured.

One method I personally have used with stakeholders is to articulate the critical success factors, or CSFs. Each is a description of a key outcome that is to be expected from a particular business function or area of interest. The 'Example Ways to Measure' column highlights some ideas of what these could be. Key performance indicators, or KPIs, can then be tagged to each CSF as the unit of measure.

This framework allows the leaders and company board to gain a better appreciation to the types of progress the organisation is making. By segmenting common and simplistic measuring criteria, this framework can also assist an organisation making that strategic journey.

As an example a business wants to organically grow its services into a new, un-tapped market. What would be the highest priority CSFs using this framework?

One CSF would be designed around 'elevate brand awareness', an obvious choice. Another would target 'raise human capital value' as the success of entering the new market hinges upon the need to retrain and retain existing staff. A third would be 'improve decision-making capabilities', as finding the best location in the new market is of utmost importance. The organisation doesn't have that existing capability. If a program is setup to organically grow these services, then a fourth CSF would obviously be 'supplemental transformational growth' to track its progress.

This scenario may be a simplistic deduction but in my working career, this type of deduction incorporating a pre-ordained measurement framework rarely, if at all, happens. Too often I have seen either a CSF scattergun approach (one's best educated guess) or even worse, a list of KPIs without any CSF anchor to the reason they exist.

In both cases the job of measuring is half complete. There are multiple measuring holes and therefore the business risks significantly rise. One example of a measuring hole is when much is left for lower management to interpret when the delivery planning activities kick in. What is prioritised and expected by the leadership may not actually occur to their liking.

The reasons why this happens are plenty. They include the usual suspects of hidden agendas, lack of accountability and poor planning governance. Perhaps though, the largest potential obstacle is the leadership.

An organisation starts and stops ultimately with its leadership. If the perception within the organisation is its leaders are not prepared or considered weak, *do not attempt* strategic planning. This will only complicate an already stressed working environment. It is important to first deal with the elephant in the room.

The leadership question

In the late 1990s just before the dot-com bubble burst, I was part of a technical team sent to Brazil. We were sent there to roll out a data warehouse and analytics project for the country's largest telecommunication (telco) companies. The project was largely funded by a US telco giant, who also had a minority share in the Brazilian telco.

The project's aim was to provide the company competitive value through the use of business intelligence data. To produce this magic data, the project had to capture good data and build an analytical reporting platform. That task largely fell to me, and a small team of technical specialists from both the US and Brazil.

The international project team got along great (hey, it's Brazil after all), and the reporting platform was tested with great success. Everything worked as expected. Our Brazilian client was happy and everyone was eager to be put what we worked for into production. On the eve of that production go-live moment, the project was killed and the platform quickly dismantled!

To say the project team was shocked was an understatement. When the truth came out, it had nothing to do with the international implementation team and everything to do with the tensions between the US-based telco sponsor (of the project) and their Brazilian management counterparts.

Someone high up in the Brazilian senior management team decided to kill the project, despite how well it had progressed. Perhaps it was a clash of egos, a lack of consultation due-diligence, petty politics or maybe a simple dislike for someone and their ideas.

Whatever the reason, over a million US dollars was lost from the project joint venture. Not to mention there were reputations scarred, recriminations pursued and the bad publicity that followed.

Everything comes back to leadership. It's no accident that at the top of the OrgPi model is management (and therefore the value of leadership). Weaknesses from a leader can easily be amplified within the organisation if the organisation allows those weaknesses to permeate out. I recently read the ability for an organisation to tolerate bad behaviours is only as strong as the leader's tolerance of them. This statement strongly resonates with me looking back at my past experiences.

With the fate of an organisation, including the value of strategic management, hanging on the performance of its leadership team, it would be remiss to exclude a discussion, 'how effective is an organisation's leadership?'

This is a question I personally like to see asked more often. Perhaps even a better question, 'what type of leader is at the helm of the organisation'? A leader who brings stability to a company, plays the key role as a company moves through a difficult period, or a stable and strong force across all business cycles?

In today's complex and interconnected functional world, it's a harder challenge than ever to be an effective leader, especially a leader of a large organisation. To be seen as someone who knows about everything within the organisation, yet also be regarded as an inspirational figurehead, all the while successfully guiding the organisation through diverse business cycles. Whew! Who would want that job?

Sometimes leaders are indeed born. I was lucky enough to know one when growing up. His name was David Taylor Jr., a close childhood friend of mine during my family's military secondment in West Germany. Even at a young age David exemplified one of those natural born leaders. He was immediately likeable, had a good temperament and was never in doubt about things. He was exceptionally good at rallying people to a cause.

Even as a kid, his rise up the leadership ladder demonstrated he was going places. First he was elected 'master patrol leader' of our scout troop. He then quickly became an Eagle Scout, the top award of a scout, at just 13, and one of the youngest ever to receive the award. He later served as class president during his senior year in high school. Following his university studies, he went into the military, like his father before him, and rose to the rank of major.

While serving in Iraq he requested to be closer to combat patrol units. It was an unusual request given his rank. It was something he did not have to do. He simply was being his inspirational, positive self.

The order was eventually approved. Those patrol troops under his command admired his tenacity and close bonds were forged. It's what any natural born leader would have done.

Sadly, in October 2006 he was killed in an IED attack on his convoy. Had it not been for that war, I have no doubt this rising, natural star would have rightfully earned his own stars to becoming a highly respectable general.

For the majority of us who are not naturally gifted with these traits, we can still acquire them throughout our life. There is a plethora of books on leadership and management to keep us busily entertained. These books contain many definitions and models made to inspire us to become better leaders.

My personal favourite describes the value of leadership in three simple tenets: 1) vision, 2) passion and 3) compassion. I've seen a similar approach describing the three as 1) vision, 2) influence and 3) trust.

Most people would equate leadership with the first two, vision and passion/influence. Entrepreneurs, for example, have plenty of vision and passion. Yet would they make effective leaders simply with these two?

Maintaining passion with other people is a tough business. It eventually fades over time if not refreshed and recalibrated. It a world of instant stimulation and information overdrive where distractions are frequent, passion only runs skin deep for many. A business's customers and potential business partners may be initially attracted by passion, but eventually want to see results to stay with the business.

Leaders need something a bit extra to sustain their influence. It's the ability to demonstrate heartfelt compassion and exhibit a strong degree of trust. The two are closely linked. It's hard to have one without the other.

Compassion is having empathy (an attribute of emotional intelligence) for what others are going through. Compassion fuels the trust factor and is both enduring and endearing to others. If passion is about purpose, compassion is about purpose with well-being intent.

It's this ability that is the defining attribute separating the top leaders from others. With compassion trust can be earned.

Speak to any leader about empathy and each will no doubt appreciate its value. Yet the key difference for a top leader is to not only have a desire to improve the situation but then individually act upon it.

Trust comes much easy under these circumstances. One example is to make it a habit to recognise and allow others to succeed before leaders do. Another example is personally demonstrating how to live the company's set of values each and every day.

What is at the heart of compassion, and how can a leader discover and strengthen this virtue? Mindfulness sits at the heart of compassion.

The ability to be mindful of one's actions leads to greater self-awareness. Self-awareness is the anchor to becoming selfless. Selflessness is an endearing, compassionate human trait.

For many decades mindfulness remained an untapped, missing ingredient from leadership discussions. That has significantly changed as plenty is written about it today. I too have already mentioned mindfulness as a mitigation technique against work busyness.

By being selfless we can increase our emotional intelligence (EI) in the process. In today's customer-driven marketplace, leaders can no longer just roll out superior widgets and feature-rich services. They need to 'connect' with their customers at a level beyond the business transaction. This is where EI comes into its own. If harnessed well, the benefits of EI are quite impressive to include stellar performance, outstanding leadership and higher levels of staff happiness.

If a leader (and their management team) is seen to be taking care of their employees, it can become a great place to work. It is *not just* a human resources function. A leader divorcing themselves from their work surroundings is making the gravest of errors.

If employees have high engagement scores at work, then this is translated to their customers. It's similar to the phrase, 'happy wife, happy life', or 'happy staff, happy customers'. Study after study demonstrates higher engagement scores leads to higher business growth.

What can a leader immediately do tomorrow to become more engaged and show a bit of mindfulness? Here are four leadership tips I have found useful through the years.

1. ***Show how to live the values of the organisation:*** *Take a values test and publish the score to the organisation. Encourage others to do the same. Most importantly highlight and publish the areas you will personally work on to strengthen your character.*

2. ***Increase qualitative time management:*** *To rid the organisation of petty discussions and time management frustrations, send out a communiqué to the organisation giving tips about how to organise a non-recurring meeting to ensure it meets expected outcomes. Live by the same creed.*

3. ***Immediately empower technology and change management business groups:*** *Compose an email around the following instructional directive: Any new innovative idea involving technology or organisational changes requires immediate inclusion of these applicable service groups. By engaging them early will change the organisational mindset from leaning on these groups in a*

reactive, blaming situation, to a more proactive and collaborative relationship. Demonstrate your confidence in these groups by sitting in on a few meetings to set the positive tone.

4. **Walk the floor:** *An oldie but goodie. Carve out an hour each week to take a trip around the building saying hello and checking in with staff. Do it once will get you noticed. Do it frequently and you will get results.*

These four tips are not intended to be game changing for the leader or the organisation, but each speaks to a leader's intent on gaining deeper awareness of their organisation. They provide a springboard to demonstrating transparency and in some cases a degree of vulnerability, both enduring compassionate traits.

From a strategy management perspective when a leader neglects to understand their workforce, this becomes one of the biggest obstacles to effectively performing strategy. Neglect is similar to turning a blind eye when it's time to perform organisational change. Too often neglect leads to the change being outsourced to someone else in the organisation. The change management difficulty level has just increased.

Some 'heads of' will knowingly divorce themselves from understanding strategic models and the use of evidence. Many may choose to do so out of fear of reprisals and other job security reasons. These individuals rationalise it is best to outsource accountability and then later claim 'I was not made aware', or 'I did not know'.

This behaviour assumes the individual trumps the organisation. It is a defensive, tactical approach based on narrow-minded, individualistic thinking. The approach may produce some immediate payoffs for the individual, but over time is quite damaging to the business. Eventually this tactic will become exposed for what it is.

To decrease this risk, it's imperative that strategic management is not neglected or outsourced from any C-level. One of the best counterweights against neglect is to have the company board jointly own the strategic plan and its execution alongside the executive management team.

A joint ownership model will tie the executive team and board together to ensure the future success of the organisation. It sounds logical but how often does this happen? A good plan is, well, only a good plan if support is not explicitly given and continually reinforced. It takes a strong leader of sound character to rally and sustain others in support of such important things.

I conclude this section with a quote from a recent Forbes article articulating the importance of having a strong and effective leader.

> *"The selection of leaders, development of leaders, and the coaching of leaders are all critical to building the right culture. Companies that focus on building great leaders spend almost 3X the average on leadership development, and they get a tremendous return for it (Bersin 2015)."*

The accountability question

Leadership discussions inevitably seem to expose some type of concern about accountability. Too much accountability, the organisation is bogged down in wasteful and inefficient processes. Too little accountability, the organisation suffers from confusion and indecision. In each case the energy and commitment levels of the workforce deteriorates over time.

Wherever my work has taken me and whatever industry I found myself in, I'm often amazed by the lack of effective business governance. The prevailing perception I've heard is this notion that qualitative business accountability has begun to diminish over the past decades. Assuming for the moment this is true and it wasn't always this poor, why and where did it go wrong?

The business world some thirty years ago generally marched to a slower drummer. Business activities were often performed with checks and counterchecks. Paper trails take time to produce, analyse and process things that matter. There was time and resources available to ensure this happened.

Eventually paper gave way to digitisation and paper trails gave way to computer automation. This meant speedier business activities could now commence.

Although has technology, as a great business disruptor, helped create half-asleep employees who do nothing more than input data and monitor transactions? Perhaps the business world has become so complex that no one really understands who is responsible for what? Perhaps it is a combination of the two or something else entirely?

Automation cuts across traditional lines of management accountability. It dilutes the understanding of roles and responsibilities as a business increases its horizontal levels of automation and efficiency gains.

There are now more dotted lines of accountability in organisation charts. As a working society we have become more adapt at multi-tasking, but poorer at making effective decisions. The engine wheel of decision-making is under increased duress.

In many conversations with management the most acute governance issue seems to sit between the inner circle of leaders (the C-team in many organisations) and management just below them. Perhaps the governance problem is just too big for any one person to adequately address. Yet nothing should be too big for a leader to tackle.

So how does a leader inspire their workforce to gain ownership of things that seem difficult? Should the leader streamline already streamlined processes, or radically reshape their management org chart to adapt to more cross-functional activities?

First step is to identify existing accountability gaps. There are a number of market tools that can already do this. One example is the RACI Matrix which has become popular during the past decade. It's a simple tool that identifies the degree of ownership for certain activities or tasks. RACI stands for the following:

R(esponsible) – Who is responsible for actually doing it?
A(ccountable) – Who has authority to approve or disapprove it?
C(onsulted) – Who has needed input about the task?
I(Informed) – Who needs to be kept informed about the task?

The governing rule with this tool is there can be only one accountable stakeholder (A), yet multiple stakeholders can be identified for the R, C and I. Many times businesses will have the R and the A shown together.

Even though this tool has gained considerable traction, I am still amazed by how little it is used within organisations. The tool comes into its own when plotting current and target-state ownership during an organisation's transformational change.

That said any tool is only as good as the environment from which it is used. The tool is great at exposing current management accountability; so poor business governance may prevent RACI from gaining traction within a project.

I personally knew a project manager refuse to use it from fear of exposing the 'accountability truth' to their project sponsor. The operational managers whom the project manager worked with wanted to play down the governance gaps. These individuals didn't want to be perceived as a weak link to why things were not working well.

Sounds crazy eh? Isn't that the whole point of running a project? Isn't it to create better efficiencies and new business value? Isn't it to reward those who need the help the most?

In this type of working environment fear and hiding the truth are normal practice. It's a type of environment where leadership could learn a few tips about how to turn around those negative attitudes.

If left unchecked a lack of accountability and ownership leads to confusion, which in turn leads to inefficiencies, chaos and reactionary business practices. These poor-performing work situations begin to affect the humanistic condition as additional work stress creeps in. As the organisation begins to buckle under the strain of ever more reactionary business practices, bad behaviours once not tolerated become increasingly unchecked.

The following chart describes these six steps that if not tackled by leadership, can eventually become fatal to an organisation. The longer it takes to address these accountabilities, a higher number of them there are.

Lack of Accountability Slippery Slope

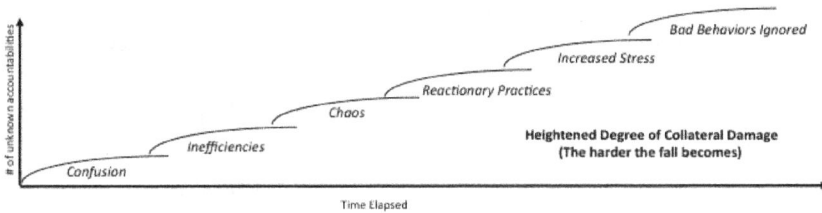

# of unknown accountabilities

Confusion

Inefficiencies

Chaos

Reactionary Practices

Increased Stress

Bad Behaviors Ignored

Heightened Degree of Collateral Damage
(The harder the fall becomes)

Time Elapsed

Contrary to popular belief bad behaviours are not simply from the actions of a few bad apples, nor is it something that happens suddenly. Studies show that bad behaviours occur gradually over time and can happen with the most well-intentioned and meaning people (Gino, Ordonez and Welsh 2014).

The situation deteriorates when people begin overlooking unethical behaviour of their peers. By choosing to ignore the behaviour they are actually condoning it. Others may rationalise it simply as a bit of 'cheating'. Though frowned upon, it is nevertheless acceptable, as they perceive it to be isolated and not really that bad.

The risk is heightened when there is no agreement or understanding to who the owner is or where the responsibility lies. A lack of accountability provides un-necessary cannon fodder to fermenting poor behaviours especially if the organisation's culture is prone to these situations.

Long-standing accountability gaps combined with a repeated disregard for ethical behaviour is a powerful combination that will seriously corrode and damage the organisation from within. The right amount of accountability mixed with supporting activities that "nudge employees in the right direction" can provide a soft landing, as opposed to a slippery slope's harder fall (Gino, Ordonez and Welsh 2014).

Accountability is not just about operational concerns; it also applies to the higher end of the business value chain. Accountability exists between shareholders, the board and the executive management team.

At this higher level within the organisation, accountability to the organisation is many times at odds from entitlements aimed at the individual. When individual value is equal or of greater weight to organisation value, this can have a significant impact on the organisation.

One obvious example is performance remuneration. When individuals are rewarded based on profitability then it is easy to lose focus on the bigger strategic picture. Tweaking that process here, adjusting this pricing strategy there to squeeze out more profits, is the preferred approach taken. It's an approach that nicely mimics an organisation's quarterly financial reporting.

An analogy I like to use is the home we choose to live in. The home provides many basic needs least of which shelter and lodging. It also provides us happiness and a sense of ownership entitlement.

The house we choose is similar to how we pick our next place of employment. Financial incentives and bonus schemes simply reinforce the notion that this is our house of employment.

Another way to describe this is that a leader's house (their business) receives constant do-it-yourself repairs (process efficiencies) and occasionally some remodelling (restructure), but rarely is an extension made, and a move to another house not even thinkable (true innovation). The profitability performance 'blinders' is holding back many businesses, giving them a reason to be more conservative in their decisions than they need be. It's a tactical game after all and their house of business has walls of steel.

These incentive schemes, as well intentioned as they are for the individual, can over time harm the organisation. The financial reward may indeed prevent that executive from leaving but that is hardly a recipe for growing the success of that business.

Yes, performing the minimal repairs necessary will keep the share price drifting upwards at a steady, manageable pace. This may satisfy both the board and shareholder community but is not a viable, long-term strategy.

Meanwhile the walls are deteriorating, the roof is leaky and those living within its walls (employees) are becoming increasingly unhappy about living there as they are asked to do more to keep the house from falling down. The hired property manager (consultancy firm) shows what could be if another house is erected, but doesn't fully appreciate the nature of the business, or its people working under its roof. Many employees have their own ideas about how to move to another house or to put in a significant extension. Unfortunately, management largely ignores those ideas instead opting to adopt the property manager's input. Good talent eventually moves away realising the organisation will never leave its house or make any significant improvements.

Making it more efficient (to live in) may be the undoing of that organisation. A tipping point to do something different is already upon many industries. Who and where is the accountability for this important evolution of the organisation?

Perhaps it is time for all businesses to re-examine their performance reward structures. It could be a performance system that doesn't prioritise the goal of producing efficiencies over producing innovation, a performance system that introduces new innovative and customer-centric pay structures into their organisation.

I would like to conclude by tying together leadership and accountability challenges. Last year I had the pleasure of attending a Conscious Capitalism conference with hundreds of business leaders. One of my takeaways was the concept of 'moral ownership', or ownership of things based on the organisation's set of values.

Moral ownership is a concept borrowed from the not-for-profit world. In those organisations 'charters' are established to provide social good to one or more communities of interest. This charter, founded on providing social value, is obviously paramount to not-for-profit organisation.

Over the past several decades, there has been a moral erosion of sorts within for-profit businesses, and today many have begun to embrace this concept of moral ownership. For some organisations moral ownership is a complimentary way of demonstrating value beyond quarterly profit reports. For others an issue like dissatisfaction from shareholders about rising executive pays might trigger it.

What can be done? One simple idea is getting more of the workforce to have a voice. To create greater buy-in that in turn will raise job satisfaction scores. Having a stronger voice will empower the workforce to want to take on greater awareness and accountability.

Another approach is to introduce values-based metrics as a significant pillar of objectivity. Human values on their own may not be measurable but they can be linked to behaviours and well-being activities that are indeed measurable.

Earlier in the book we explored how social value, once immeasurable, is becoming measurable and accepted in the corporate world. Global initiatives such as B-Corp, B-Team and Conscious Capitalism all continue to trumpet the success of socially-based enterprises. This moral ownership concept might finally become a major anchor between balancing effective leadership and accountability throughout the business value chain.

Re-positioning the management consultant

Heard the latest consultant joke? "If you see a consultant on a bicycle, why should you be extra careful not to hit him? It might be your bicycle." As someone who spent considerable time in the consulting field, I can attest to consultant colleagues who do more than simply advise how to ride it. Many choose to get on the bike and take it for a 'business spin'.

However not all consultants are created the same and not all management consultancy firms are necessarily as bad as they are made out to be. It's easy to find many consultant-bashing books so I promise to not repeat this trend here. Yes, consultants can indeed provide value to organisations in many ways. The trick is to understand how best to employ their services to maximum your business value.

Thinking back to my years on the consultant road there was one thing that struck me no matter where I was assigned. Each consulting firm I worked for was good at explaining to clients what their competitors were up to where their industry was headed. As Michael Porter wrote, "consultants flood the market with information about what other companies are doing, reinforcing the best practice mentality (Porter, Kim and Mauborgne 2011, 29)."

The logic went that if a business just followed this approach (like others before it), it could stay competitive and realise x growth on its returns.

This assumes one fundamental principle: there is a natural progression to a company's maturity that can somehow be equated to its profitability. Improve this process over here, acquire that asset over there and costs will go down to stay competitive.

In the Kaizen business world this made perfect sense. Today however why would a business leader pay a hefty service fee to a big consultancy firm to simply follow best practice? Isn't the primary aim of today's competitive landscape to differentiate the organisation's unique value to customers? To separate itself from the myriad of competitors?

This best practice approach, important as it is, is not the chief driver in today's customer-centric competitive environment. The main challenge is finding innovative ways to attract new customers whilst ensuring existing customers remain loyal. Business innovation is based on competitive uniqueness, or new ways to differentiate, not industry standard approaches.

Another misperception is who should qualify as a strategist. Having the smartest person in the room, usually in the form of a consultant, does not increase chances of success. In fact, it may be the wrong approach.

Studies show that the smarter someone is, the more inclined they are to problem-solve in search of the right answer. In a world of strategic trade-offs where there is no clear right answer, strategic thinking may not be the right environment for smart people. In an essay appropriately entitled 'Why smart people struggle with strategy', Roger Martin argues "there is no way to determine that one's strategy choice was 'right', because there is no way to judge the relative quality of any path against all the paths not actually chosen (Martin 2014)."

Strategic thinking requires a good dose of common sense coupled with an acute awareness of different business angles. High IQs need not apply. With plenty of smart people working in management consultancy firms, giving a firm a blank check to help find the right strategic plan for an organisation may do more harm than good.

That is not to say there isn't value in using a room of smart management consultancy people. Smart people execute complex things quite well.

Given a defined set of parameters in which to perform, consultants offer high value during their client engagement. Certain types of consultancy services such as performing audits, implementing a complex business system rollout, and conducting targeted research, all offer the promise of delivering tangible and necessary business value.

For example, if a business is searching for a new direction and strategy to pursue, they may seek insights from targeted research to better understand what their competitors are doing before choosing their path. Having this information can help create real business value.

If, however, the client asks the consultancy firm for advice on a preferred strategic direction, this is where the value becomes diluted. Naturally the consultancy firm is only so happy to help – after all, the business client has asked for this and is ready to hear someone's advice. It's not the firm's fault that the advice may not be well received. All they have to deliver are best-fit options based on existing best practices, and deliver them in the most professional and polite way possible, so as to not offend.

This is where I differ from others I speak to who think management consultancy firms are evil and dastardly. These firms are just fulfilling a request, be it naïve, from the business.

Imagine the day when management consultancy firms had strategic performance metrics tied to the organisation's growth or profitability instead of delivering an expected service for a fixed period of time. Now that would be a completely different engagement model to consider. Given the business world has moved away from an operational efficiency model to a customer-centric one then shouldn't the consultancy engagement also inherently change?

The responsibility for innovating a new engagement model shouldn't fall upon the established management consultancy firms. They will only modify their business practices when there is a strong enough desire and demand.

The demand starts with businesses that seek a new consultancy relationship tied closer to mutual business outcomes. Like any competitive industry, consultancy firms who are nimble can position themselves to offer unique innovative value quite different to simply assisting with operational efficiencies.

Exploring the enterprise architect & change manager roles

Many of you reading may be asking, 'what the hell is an Enterprise Architect or Change Manager?' If my career had not intersected with these roles I would be wondering the same thing.

In the many years working as an enterprise architect, or EA practitioner, I struggled to succinctly explain what it is that I did, especially to senior executives. The same was true for many of my fellow EA colleagues. Join any enterprise architect discussion group and it's easy to see why.

Nearly the same experience and identity issue can be found with the field of change management. I'm still astounded by the number of senior business executives that believe it's just a fancy term for training or communications to staff on the latest technology rollouts.

The enterprise architect role has its foundations in technology design and process change impact. The change manager's skill sets are founded upon understanding the human condition as it adapts to environmental changes in the workplace.

Both roles have a common thread. They are critical in formulating a strategic roadmap and monitoring the progress of its execution.

They each deliver organisation-wide value by working across multiple business groups. This ability to have far-reaching visibility and organisational insights is a rarity for roles that are not C-level.

If these roles do not have senior executive and board member visibility, then what hope is there a successful strategic execution will occur? It's for this reason that I wanted to include these two misunderstood but critical roles in this book.

First up is the EA role. This role is just over a decade old. It was created in many organisations during the early part of the 2000s as a reaction to ensure better design control and strategic decision making within the IT department. This was a period of time just following the dot-com bust, Y2K and major corporate collapses like Enron and MCI WorldCom. Controlling the delivery value of IT departments was the hot topic of the day.

Since that time the EA role has shifted closer to a business-oriented value role. A role that enables organisations to better fit their technology and business decisions to maximise investment value. It has morphed into what I would summarise as a 'technology-meets-business strategist' rather than a pure designer or builder of technology systems.

Many enterprise architects today still wear these two different hats, the older internal IT improvement hat and the newer hat that delivers higher business value. One is more technical than the other. Begin to see the confusion forming?

The technical IT improvement hat is more about the 'how'. It is solution building. The business value hat is more about the 'why' and 'what'. It is more strategic than solution delivery.

To deliver good design, or the how, it's necessary to have a good understanding of the 'what' and 'why' first. The traditional roles of the business analyst and project manager, important as these roles are, have been ill equipped to capture what and why effectively.

As I covered earlier in the section, 'Rethinking Project Delivery Governance' the job was left to the architect to question things that should have been questioned earlier in the planning phase. This usually caused un-necessary tension between the project delivery team and the architect from the IT department. Over time the EA, who was not tied to specific projects, began to step into this organisational need to better understand the 'what' and 'why'.

The potential benefits of an EA role are enormous to an organisation. As the role is organisation-wide, an EA has access to identify and capture internal business trends and pains from numerous areas within the organisation. These could include a range of diverse things like inadequate system training support, and a lack of information security protocols to better protect the business from external and internal privacy threats.

A good EA can assist the leadership team in consolidating and prioritising these diverse needs into a rationalised and measured approach. This approach runs counter to the older silo capital planning method of 'who shouts loudest wins' from amongst the various business units. In another words, the EA is positioned as one of the key experts in formulating a strategic execution plan.

In one organisation I worked for my team and I each year would sit down in numerous one-on-one sessions with business directors from diverse areas of the business. In each session we captured a list of things they wished or needed to tackle in the coming financial year. Many of these items were not technology-specific. Some items were tactical, operational improvements and others quite innovative in scale and ambition.

The next step of the planning process involved our team analysing what was possible given the state of many business systems across the organisation. We just didn't analyse the technology value, but also the people and process fit.

Our team then drafted a set of proposed action items that each director could achieve with our technology assistance. Sometimes we could deliver exactly what they wanted and in other cases, based on the evidence we collected, they needed to improve upon a particular business area first.

The final stage was to sit down with each and have a discussion about what was achievable and by when. A final list of agreeable, achievable actions was written into an executive report and submitted to the executive management team for final endorsement.

The entire process was collaborative and educational between both technology and business leadership. We made the executive report an evidence-based report accessible to everyone in the organisation. The transparency in the planning process and subsequent release of the reports engendered a positive and engaging atmosphere for all involved. As a final step, each year we would monitor and report on the progress of all the formalised actions.

I earlier said 'potential benefit' as the challenge is how to better structure an organisation to take advantage of this strategic asset. There are a few common issues to consider here.

One potential issue is attempting to create a single EA role that tries to do too much. Asking someone to address the big three of why, what and how is putting too much influence and responsibility into a single role.

Having too much thought leadership in one role is not only a reputational risk for that individual but also for the organisation that employs them. It becomes too diluted and more difficult to manage across a diverse set of stakeholders. Many client stakeholders can become confused as to exactly who they are and what they represent.

I know this all too well from past experiences. Here is just a snippet of things I've heard throughout the years whilst working as an EA:

- *Shouldn't we ask that person... what's their title again?*

- *Why is that person challenging what we've already decided we're going to do?*

- *Shouldn't he simply confirm we could build what we want?*

- *Why does technology have to be so hard?*

- *I can never understand what those architects say when they speak.*

Recognise a pattern here? Another issue usually stems from one simple reason – the EA role does not have a clear mandate or access across the organisation. Historically the role has been created from within the IT department as a way to enhance the IT department's reputation and value.

As virtuous and noble a cause this may be, it still misses the point. Why should an EA spend an enormous amount of energy selling their strategic value to the greater business community?

If the role doesn't have buy-in from the top, then the role will be perceived as just the latest concoction from the IT department. The

EA targeted audience may not fully welcome their arrival, especially if the IT department is struggling to achieve greater buy-in. The message that a technology strategist requires a true business planning partnership with their stakeholders can be a tough sell for many.

To help sell the role at the top level, Forrester Research recently dubbed a new leadership role as the Chief Business Technology Officer, or CBTO. The newly appointed CBTO of Forrester (a case of practice what you preach) described his new role in an interview with Robert Plant as follows: "helping define and drive our business strategy, as well as being responsible for how we use technology to 'win, serve, and retain' customers (Plant 2014)."

I once sat down with a director who explained to me their inorganic growth strategy was based on acquiring a number of existing facilities all of which were poorly performing. Interestingly the group's primary vision was to organically build new, innovative facilities in highly sought after locations they had already researched. These new facilities required heavy capital injection and some of that source could come from the newly acquired facilities.

The first business priority was to quickly assimilate those facility acquisitions. The main problem was the slow, time-intensive acquisition process. A large issue was not enough administrative staff to cope with the acquisitions. The acquiring facilities were also leery to come on board with a small administrative support staff.

My team quickly identified a number of simple technology-based assets the administrative team could immediately begin using. Gaining access to and learning the new systems and processes wouldn't require the need to run a formal project to deliver these new assets.

In a short three-month period, our team significantly enhanced the admin team's performance by simply allowing access to existing technology services their team did not make use of. The administrative team gained quick confidence in these new tools and their performance levels significantly increased. More importantly, the facilities being acquired had greater confidence to become integrated quicker than originally intended.

This increased administrative capacity and performance (at no additional cost and without having to hire more resources) meant the business group could move forward its acquisition targets. This also meant they could move forward their plans to organically grow in markets previously identified.

I'll expose you to a little known industry secret. Those enterprise architects, who have some fifteen or more years of experience working across a number of different industry verticals, can understand your business better than you might think. Two primary reasons for this is that many of the toughest business and technology challenges tend to be the same no matter what industry it is.

A seasoned EA who has broad industry reach can add significantly higher value than finding someone who only has experience in a particular industry niche. They can give a fresh, independent perspective to a business model. These days why would anyone hire an expensive management resource that is only good at tweaking a business to stay with the competition?

A similar example is those CEOs who traverse industry to industry to lead a business they have never been a part of. How is it that these individuals can do that? They tend to have a broad base of experience and are highly desired. They are known as successful leaders. A good EA with a similar reputation operates in much the same way providing value for an organisation.

Much of it comes down to having a high degree of inter-personal skills to be successful. This is also absolutely critical for the role of a Change Manager.

So who are change managers? Much like EA role ambiguity, there is much variation in their form and function of change management. One truism does exist; change management tackles an organisation's adaptability to things.

In a complex operating environment full of interlocking systems and processes the value of change management can be quite profound, but what exactly is it? Much like an enterprise architect, a change manager analyses the current and future states to help determine what is needed to get the organisation from their current state to the new future state.

The people who are employed by an organisation are a change manager's primary focus. The internationally established change management institute, Prosci, defines change management as: the application of a structured process and set of tools for leading the people side of change to achieve a desired outcome (Prosci 2015).

It is clear that these days' organisations of all types are constantly going through some degree of change. It could be from either an internal desire to change something or because of an external force affecting the organisation. It may be changes to computer systems, a product or service they sell, or how they operate.

Organisations cannot change something that affects their employees and simply say 'just do it this way now'. Many have tried this approach without much success; particularly in environments where there has been a lot of change occurring. There are strong industry statistics showing the success of changes delivered where there have been change management processes used as opposed to those that did not.

Change managers can be utilised for a particular project or at a wider organisational level. From personal experience I have stopped counting the number of times I have heard the argument, 'it's just a technology change there is no people change'. A change manager would immediately respond with, 'but who uses the technology? It is people, so the change involves *how people* will use that technology.'

Why bother to build or upgrade the best systems if no one wants to use them, doesn't know how to use them, or simply resist? The time and energy spent fighting user battles can easily blow out project budgets and can foster the introduction of bad behaviour within the organisation. Technology is just a channel of disgruntlement for something else gone awry.

To combat this, a change manager works closely with the business to develop solutions to get people on board with as little resistance as possible. This work includes identifying potential areas of resistance that can be mitigated or monitored.

Throughout the process of implementing change, details are continually refined by always challenging the question, 'what will this mean for those impacted by the change?' The change manager helps ensure those affected by the change understand the following:

- Why *the change is being made,*
- How *the change is being implemented,*
- *The* 'What's in it for me?' *Or the* benefits *of the change*
- How *to do things the* new way,
- Embed *the change by continuing to* stay with the new way *of doing things.*

Some key activities in change management practice include impact and readiness assessments, communications, training, and strategic plans to ensure the change is accepted.

Like the EA role, there are a number of challenges within change management practice. Perhaps the first one is to understand if we are talking about technology change management or organisation change management. Technology departments use 'change management' but in a completely different way.

IT change management has to do with how technology components are managed from one version to the next. The quite complex world of technology with its many moving parts requires close management scrutiny of all those components as they move from planning to development, then to test and finally to deployment.

Naturally this type of change management has very little to do with organisational or people change management. I encourage senior management to be aware of this difference when discussing any governance and provisioning of IT assets.

Another challenge continues to be an educational one. A number of business leaders still consider change management as nothing more than a training or communications plan required for staff. This completely misses the core value of change management to the organisation.

The discipline continues to suffer from an awareness issue that in turn hides the enormous benefits that can be derived from it. This situation is similar to the EA role where many think enterprise architects simply design and build things.

Once again it takes recognition from the top leadership to endorse change management value. Without this support, change managers have to fight to win over various stakeholders across the organisation. When existing change management champions choose to exit the organisation, the fight continues, as the educational process must start over again with their replacements. The time and energy spent can be quite exhausting over the years.

Gaining recognition and endorsement from the executive management team is absolutely critical. It ensures not only the survival of the change management practice, but eliminates the need for change managers to continually have to defend their value.

Senior execs that explicitly endorse change management value grant those teams the ability to enact the program they have proposed and devised. The team essentially has a 'green light' from the top to do what they do best as experts. A plan unencumbered from any subsequent management dilution of their value. With the green light also comes full responsibility and liability for that change.

This approach demonstrates top leadership priority, seriousness and recognition of change management to facilitate and drive the change. Boards would only be too happy to know their executive management team supports and backs with confidence an army of change agents to help facilitate this organisational journey. In many cases just a simple statement of authority is all that is needed for those change agent troops going into the front line of the change battle.

In summarising this section, I often say having a good EA and a good change manager who work well together can perform wonders for that organisation. They are an absolute must-have for major transformation programs. The earlier they are brought on board, the better.

The ultimate aim should be about reorienting the organisation's capability to compete better. Each of these roles is pivotal in that journey, yet each brings unique organisational perspectives to the management and delivery of that strategic initiative.

Magic truly begins to happen when these roles are elevated in their exposure at the top of the leadership command. When elevated, the organisation is implicitly elevating the human condition and technology as key drivers of strategic change.

The business governance question

If you're a board member, then this section may be of particular interest. Over the years I've come to appreciate some of the weighty questions occupying a board's time. Questions such as, does the company have the right management team to consider the monumental business changes afoot? Does the executive team collectively work together in formulating strategy? What contingencies are there should there be leadership changes during the rollout of its strategy?

As illustrated throughout this book, strategic decision-making needs to evolve away from a world once dominated by operational efficiencies and specialisation. Strategy needs to have a broader organisational mandate. In a new world where consumer quality reigns supreme, there is no other alternative approach.

For organisations with deeply embedded ways of operating, a leader cannot simply wave a magic wand to unwind decades of business practices and cultural attitudes. Breaking down barriers reinforced by diverse and independent functioning business units is no easy task. Perhaps even more challenging is shifting the mindset and performance structure from just driving costs down to new drivers such as customer loyalty and user experience.

Business silos and cultural norms designed around process improvements obviously have a significant impact on the way a business manages complex operational issues. These situations usually take up the bulk of time and effort within management. Complex operational issues usually stretch across multiple business groups (otherwise known as cross-functional business activities). It's amazing that anything gets done given the amount of time and effort it can take to change an end-to-end process.

When situations become too complex to manage, historically it meant specialists were then brought in to help manage the complexity. Perhaps this is an area where business governance can begin to align itself for the new business age?

In the context of a labour workforce, the opposite of specialisation is generalisation. A generalist has common knowledge about many things. How they choose to use that knowledge defines their ability to effectively perform.

The time has arrived for businesses to champion a generalist over a crack team of specialists, or subject-matter experts. I suppose this may sound a bit counter-intuitive to our traditional thinking. I'm reminded for a moment about the art of skiing being counter-intuitive. (I've been an avid skier for much of my life.)

The steeper the slope, the more a skier should lean into it downhill, not uphill. Leaning the body downhill actually slows one from going faster. Yet it's counter-intuitive.

Our brains think cognitively if we lean back (or up the hill) we should be able to stop quicker as our bodies seem to be closer to the ground. Conversely this weight distribution to the back of the skis sends us down the hill faster. Instead of applying this logic, I unfortunately had to learn the hard way how to ski by practicing some terrible spills, strained muscles and a few near misses with trees I'd rather forget.

This counter-intuitive, generalist approach is exactly what businesses require today in a world where everything seems to have been flipped on its head.

Life has indeed become too complex and as the pace of change quickens, so too does the need for ever-quicker decision making within an organisation. Business cycles have shortened to days (and in some cases hours) where not long ago these cycles would have taken months. More is also being asked of boards to signify a changing of the times.

What is needed today are people capable of simplifying complex topics so that decision making is more relevant and effective; people who can also be innovative and collaborative.

There are times when a generalist has a distinct advantage over a specialist. They are more adept to thinking 'outside of the box'. A generalist, witnessing a multitude of experiences and having broad knowledge, can borrow ideas and concepts from multiple places and join these together to create something quite new and innovative.

The concept of 'design thinking' illustrates this generalist way of thinking. Though the concept has been around since the 1970s it has recently re-emerged to become an effective source for thought leadership.

It specifically draws upon empathy, rationality and yes, creativity to construct a more powerful design or solution. In particular, it's the use of empathy that makes it a powerful and creative force for intended target groups as well as for the 'design thinking' participants. I really enjoy this rationale from Dr. Paddi Lund:

"Customers don't buy from anyone unless they see benefits to themselves. Business owners don't run a business if there is no profit. Why should we think that the principles of motivation work any differently for the people in the business team (Lund 1997, 9)?"

A generalist puts together a set of best options from amongst differing organisational forces. Whereas a specialist tends to see the scientific side of things in how they fit together as a series of components or processes, a generalist can cut through this technical noise and apply relevance to a more human condition approach. Quickly getting to the heart of a business matter best suits the generalist over the specialist who is prone to a detailed analysis-paralysis situation.

A seasoned generalist simplifies complex topics, applies equal rigour to multiple competing and diverse forces, sees the big picture by thinking laterally, and is able to perform their role at a higher efficiency rate than a team of specialists. A generalist, if supported with appropriate governance measures, can help the organisation better compete. Who said the generalist was a dying breed?

I believe there is a truism today that can shed light to finding a better governance path. With some seven billion of us (and counting) on this planet, it's hard to avoid bumping into each other.

Part of my childhood was spent in Colorado. My family would often make camping trips into the nearby mountains almost anywhere we wanted. We were isolated enough that we would never come across or hear from a stranger during each trip. Just two decades later when I returned to live in Colorado, it was harder to find such a place. The state's population had nearly doubled since my childhood days. Finding a place of solitude is becoming more and more challenging.

The world indeed might appear to be shrinking as our population soars, but we are also becoming more connected to each other in the process. The introduction of the Internet and subsequent social media explosion has in large ways accelerated that process. Our tendency to thirst for knowledge and our innate curiosity are powering and strengthening those social bonds.

Organisations who are better at tapping into this connected, smaller world gain considerable wealth and internal benefits. The inverse of not doing this is perhaps even scarier.

As repeatedly demonstrated it takes just a single negative comment from a consumer about a company to have potentially global consequences. The same holds true for a current or former employee.

For example, a disgruntled employee can be venting about something at work outside of their work environment. They have their brand damaging rant recorded (unknowingly) by a stranger with their iPhone. The stranger then amusingly uploads it to their Facebook account for a laugh. The video goes viral, a crisis erupts at the organisation, and the public relations squad is called in for damage control. Those fifteen minutes of Facebook fame translates into one to two quarters of slower than expected financial growth, as consumers shy away from associating themselves with that brand.

When I was a teenager I grew up in West Germany during the height of the Cold War. I remember watching poorly acted-out commercials put together by the Armed Forces Network, or AFN. The most memorable one I recall was from their 'think OPSEC' series of commercials. It featured a few enlisted men in a local bar talking about their joint military operation. In the booth next to them was a trench coat wearing, shadowy figuring who was taking notes about their conversation.

The art of eaves dropping will never change but the scale and speed to which it affects people and organisations is unparalleled. Don't think this will happen to your business? Think again.

Nearly every day some company is named and shamed from a plethora of mainstream media channels. They pick up their feeds from what's trending online. The days of quietly flying under the publicity radar are now a thing of the past.

Wait a minute. What about those multiplying and grievous security threats also facing every organisation? There is just so much more to consider in today's dynamic customer environment.

Governance mechanisms based on 'command and control' management styles are inadequately positioned to tackle an infinite amount of unknown business scenarios. Just ask the military who are finding it hard to combat the emerging cyber war threats.

Militaries are built for a single purpose, to fight (and win) wars. Ground, air and sea battles are based on move and countermove situations that are role-played and scenario tested. Yet in the cyber war frontier, many times you don't know who and where your enemy is. This makes it difficult to predict the enemy's next moves. Not to mention the location of the next attack can change to any arbitrary place on the planet at a moment's notice.

In today's challenging business climate, command and control mechanisms are simply not adaptable and responsive enough to meet the new competitive demands. A number of reasons include:

- *A structure and philosophy originally designed for management redundancy and thoroughness;*

- *The promise of a long career into the top ranks of the organisation;*

- *Modelled around rewarding individual performance and efficiency;*

- *Supported and anchored by an army of specialists who perform a range of unique roles, and thereby thwart an organisation's potential for truly innovating.*

It's time to consider another approach.

Moving beyond business silos and their operational efficiencies

Returning to the theme of the book, the problem remains not with the thinking side of strategy but the inadequate implementation of it. A contributing factor is too many separate business units independently operating in their own business silos.

In the Kaizen business world where process efficiencies defined the competitive landscape, having an organisation-wide strategic plan was of little value. Business silos were more or less encouraged. Each silo worked in isolation and those business units who succeeded at it, attracted larger market growth. Those that didn't were dismantled or sold off. The business world inhaled and exhaled in a predictable manner.

Looking back, times did seem a bit simpler. (The warped value of hindsight.) If we were to peer under the business covers, we would discover each silo generally had a duplication of data and business processes. Over the past several decades the rise of corporate service groups (or shared service models) have somewhat dented the duplication of data and business practices, but yet the influence of silos still largely remains. These silos today are major obstacles to a leader's ability to lead a transformation, and for an organisation to successfully execute a strategic transformation program of work.

In smaller, entrepreneurial organisations there are no business silos to weaken the governance of the business at large. Their smaller market size, less complicated operating models, and detailed business cases largely protect them against the silo bug. Are silos just a naturally occurring consequence once an organisation becomes large enough?

In a start-up organisation it is paramount to have a continual review and refinement of its strategy. This review keeps not only the business afloat and competitive in the early stages of its growth, it also keeps the investors happy by keeping expectations in line with growth forecasts.

To attract investors entrepreneurs are usually asked to develop a litany of things like: a detailed business plan, marketing strategy, investment strategy and implementation plan. That's a lot of documents and hours spent thinking and planning the new business. The planning thoroughness is many times higher than in businesses that are ten times larger.

Why shouldn't a larger business do the same thing if it is looking to change or alter its current business direction? Why not perform the same steps an entrepreneur would go through? Today the closest comparison of an entrepreneurial attempt can be found when submitting a particular business solution.

Business solutions deliver point in time, discrete value to a business silo. Solutions are usually built on top of previous solutions like a stack of Jenga. In silo-based organisations much of the value from delivering these solutions is not linked to the larger organisation. These solutions are not strategic by nature.

When opportunities to strategically reuse a solution elsewhere are identified, many times the solution was not designed to be scalable. Project costs and time pressures often thwart an attempt to make that original business solution scalable. So it becomes quite expensive to retrofit it elsewhere.

There are also accountability issues that can cloud strategic value intent. The vertical decision-making apparatus of a silo does not lend well to cross-functional value gain.

A mid-level manager's desire to tap into a solution from another business group must require consent from higher up management in both business groups, as well as oversight and review from a corporate service group (like IT, Human Resources and Finance). The time and energy it takes to link value together is often times harder than the expected value gained from a good fit transaction.

How to begin breaking down these barriers? One of the keys to creating higher solution value is gaining a deeper appreciation of the 'what' before discussing the 'when', 'who' and 'how'. (For more details refer to the OrgPi model in the section, 'No more stupid strategic execution'.)

Too many times in my career I've seen poor project planning stemming from poor quality of business analysis. Projects tend to only record detailed business processes without knowing or fully understanding the fundamental business capabilities. The little that is recorded during the analysis phase either is too technical (to not be relevant), or too detailed that it misses the ability to demonstrate traceable business value back to the strategic aims of the project.

The assumed business knowledge remains either locked away in someone's head or is never captured and appropriately vetted. This unfortunate situation where there is no traceable business value later surfaces during project delivery, leading to all manner of project complications not previously envisioned.

Then there's the classic knock-on effect. Not adequately capturing the business value prevents others who sit outside the business group from fully appreciating the business impact to their own business group. A strategist, enterprise architect and change manager, however, will appreciate the wider organisational value attached. They have broader awareness to how these capabilities may affect other business units.

Why not encourage organisation-wide discussions and input *before* any business group's project scope is formally locked in? This simple change in process would encourage wider buy-in across the organisation and thereby decrease the likelihood of a business silo acting independently.

These pre-project conversations are redirecting the value beyond a business group's operational efficiency needs. There's deep discussion about what it means to the organisation and its wider impact on a strategic initiative. The right conversations are happening at the right time.

This conservation redirection has a downstream impact on when and how project briefs and work requests are submitted. There needs to be a closer planning partnership between the central planning group and the various heads of. Only then will silo decision-making influence begin to wane.

Let's compare this model to that of the earlier mentioned start-up. The entrepreneur is of course the leader, but they are also the strategist and change manager. In a start-up, the entrepreneur knows their business inside and out. The investors are the business's heads of, each trying to ply their financial influence on the start-up.

In a larger organisation the leader simply cannot know it all. So who then governs the various internal business plans and investor strategies?

If an organisation does not invite their strategists and change managers to an early business conversation, then these documents (project business cases and briefs) would suffer from a lack of cohesiveness and organisation-wide value. The same obviously holds true where there are no strategists and change managers within the organisation.

This conversation redirection should especially apply to those proposed big and complex business solutions. These projects naturally require more thinking and planning to increase the chances for success. That said, the conversation should also apply to those perceived lighter-weight solutions as well.

For these reasons organisations should reduce the sheer number of big and complex projects. The focus instead should be on increasing the number of smaller and agile-like projects.

Taking this principled approach can isolate and diminish the influence of silo thinking by attacking the very thing it feeds from, complexity and governance indecisiveness. Cross-functional, small and more agile projects create value with minimal risk and disruption. These simply need to ensure they are linked to the end game and all the bits of the strategic puzzle fit together.

Suppose I'm the head of a large company where I throw my explicit support behind a customer-centric strategic initiative. I would want to know how each of my business units adopts their own delivery plan that aligns with this initiative. I'm definitely not the expert here so I'm going to call upon my own strategists and change managers who know more about my business. I want them to work with those heads of to ensure the highest level of successful delivery to the strategic initiative. My chief risk is the 'too big to fail' project mentality as it will derail the need to turn out quick results as part of my company's customer transformation.

There are other attributes to business silo entrenchment such as financial delegate authority, capital-planning procedures and of course, reporting lines. These structural, procedural and policy barriers can and should be reset within the journey to dismantling silo support structures.

This section uncovered two main themes. The first was to arm the leader to use strategic thought leaders within the delivery side, and second to highlight delivery value from more business agile and flexible approaches. Both of these are powerful elements to taming the silo beast and it would be remiss to not mention business agility in more detail.

Agility everywhere

The expression 'business agility' is just about everywhere you look at the moment. I need not introduce or define its value, but let's just say that agility has something to do with quickly changing in response to customer behaviour and markets.

Business agility is often misinterpreted as faster delivery of operational tweaks in the business. Quickly adapting to customer changes and operational efficiency tweaks are not necessarily the same thing.

Visualise for a moment a board meeting where the members have been associated with the organisation for decades. They glance at a board report stating how the organisation has improved 10% of its least efficient processes to lay claim of being more agile. They all nod in agreement that their executive team has met this target and can perform with agility. Satisfied, they move to the next agenda item.

This scenario is nothing more than old world thinking about how businesses compete. The board in this scenario completely misses the point and can actually cause more harm to the organisation. How? The organisation is meandering about the operational efficiency game, all the while losing its focus on critical market share.

Yes, being more agile will require changes to existing business processes but at its heart, agility is a business state of mind requiring a cultural transformation.

Have you come across this type of comment? 'That particular business group will never change their way. We've tried everything and it will just not happen'.

It continues to amaze me in these situations management never thought of asking expert advice from a change manager. I suppose therein lies the problem. Management has made the dangerous assumption that 'we know our people best so therefore we should just accept this perspective and try something else'.

Perhaps they have tried before and failed. Therefore, they say it's too much to ask. How can an organisation increase its customer value when it doesn't wish to pursue what its own people are capable of?

Business agility needs to be buttressed by new supporting 'artefacts' as Edgar Schein called them (when we examined his work in the section, 'Revisiting the importance of an organisation's cultural identity'). This requires re-evaluating existing cultural values and underlying assumptions. Only then can the organisation introduce new governance mechanisms and other artefacts to support this new agile operating environment.

Business agility is not just about developing the right state of mind. It's also about building new technology and business best practices as well. Are there any ground rules to becoming agile?

One rule is technology should not be delivered in isolation from the business requirements. Another rule is that it should not be *the* key driver to being more agile. From my many years spent as an IT consultant I unfortunately recall countless projects that applied one of these two rules. In nearly every case, the project failed to deliver to expectations.

Without one or more business representatives closely guiding the delivery, neither approach will succeed in being more business agile. Technology should be viewed as a delivery channel, not the remedy.

The agility magic potion is the tight interplay between business value and the role of technology in delivering better responsiveness and optimum results. Business and technology elements are interwoven into the delivery approach. Otherwise the expected customer experience will not have been tested before rolling out the solution into production. The art of solution testing is central to being agile.

To reduce solution complexity there might be a number of smaller business changes that don't need a formal delivery structure. They can instead be accomplished through business-as-usual activities (BAU), flying under the radar so to speak. These decisions should be vetted and scrutinised well before they are de-scoped from the formal delivery path.

I tend to find these BAU opportunities are often missed in the planning stages. The quick adaptation approach of business agility creates and fosters an environment for finding new clever ways to break up the complexity and timeframe in executing a strategic initiative.

I'm reminded of someone once saying, 'view things as short-term instead of long-term. Long-term things are harder to reach as a goal.' Agile thinking is about breaking pieces of work into bite sized, easy to manage pieces. This is the essence of agile thinking and it's a fantastic recipe for strategic transformation initiatives.

CHAPTER 7:

Meeting the Challenges of Today

"For at least the past decade, managers have been preoccupied with improving operational effectiveness... And bit by bit, management tools have taken the place of strategy. As managers push to improve on all fronts, they move farther away from viable competitive positions... Continuous improvement has been etched on managers' brains. But its tools unwittingly draw companies toward initiation and homogeneity. Gradually, managers have let operational effectiveness supplant strategy. The result is zero-sum competition, static or declining prices, and pressures on costs that compromise companies' ability to invest in the business for the long term."

- Michael Porter, What is Strategy?

Operational efficiencies continue to occupy a leader's attention as much, if not more, than their ability to think strategically. This legacy way of thinking compromises the most important discussions that should be taking place more often.

This chapter addresses real-world challenges and offers possible opportunities where strategic management can be more effectively used. In doing so it attempts to chip away at the efficiency-thinking juggernaut.

For those reading this who see their organisation at the beginning of this journey, it's my hope these opportunities can be your 'starting blocks' to becoming more strategic and less reactive. For those who have already started to make significant changes, I've included eight sections in this chapter to choose where you can find additional value. Each section tackles a unique challenging area.

Throughout this chapter I've tried to provide examples to what others are thinking and doing. Obviously not all these challenges are relevant to each and every business hence presenting eight areas instead of a few.

I've provided a summary of these eight sections in presentational order. It's meant as a reference guide in case you immediately wish to jump to a particular challenge. (**BC** = Business Challenge, **PS** = Proposed Solution)

1. Classifying capital to better align with strategic management

- *   **BC:** *My business is under tremendous pressure from shareholders to maintain profit margins. As a result, charting a new course remains a secondary priority at the moment.*

- *   **PS:** *Begin segmenting and tracking your various forms of capital more efficiently to help achieve both goals.*

2. ## The power of a business blueprint for capital planning

- *BC: My business has problems tracking the strategic value of the activities it wishes to initiate.*

- *PS: Consider an annual business roadmap to link proposed initiatives to strategic objectives, to include integrating roadmap into a capital planning process.*

3. ## Co-dependencies, marketing versus technology

- *BC: My business requires greater knowledge about our customers to make more effective decisions on where we take our business.*

- *PS: Consider aligning closer governance and work practices between your CIO and CMO heads.*

4. ## The value of a semi-permanent business change group

- *BC: We have difficulty in transforming our business. Though we understand we need to change, we are weary that we will repeat the same mistakes of the past.*

- *PS: Consider establishing a business change group that is augmented by a special advisory board to ensure effective management of that change.*

5. ## Rethinking those rusty and outdated organisational pipes

- *BC: My business is mired in management approval overhead taxing our ability to effectively execute change well.*

- *PS: Consider replacing those old vertical management lines with more horizontally driven approaches and techniques.*

6. ## The use of brokering services as a new approach

- *BC: We want to develop an in-house strategy group but lack initial capital and expertise to fund one.*

- *PS: Consider using a brokering service that acts as an effective bridge to win over board support whilst ensuring you capture top talent in the process.*

7. <u>Rediscovering the art of corporate social responsibility</u>

- **BC:** *My business is having difficulty attracting top talent to stay competitive.*

- **PS:** *Consider integrating social capital initiatives but with a new twist – to create a powerful change with purpose.*

8. <u>Mimicking entrepreneurs to become innovative</u>

- **BC:** *My business is not seen as very innovative but we need to be, and though we have tried, many of our innovations are simply not good ideas.*

- **PS:** *Begin thinking and being more entrepreneurial by using similar engagement models of practice.*

Classifying capital to better align with strategic management

When sitting my accountancy course a number of years ago, I remember covering was the concept of 'capital'. At the time I didn't fully appreciate the significance of this term.

From my experiences as an entrepreneur, architect and strategist, I have since come to understand the nature of capital at a deeper level. In researching this book I am only beginning to comprehend just how important the definition is to the future world of business.

What strikes me most is lack of understanding and often times a misrepresentation to how capital is managed. There are the 'working', 'recovery', and 'budgeting' forms of capital to name a few. Each differs in the way they are applied within an organisation.

For example, take working capital. There is no clear application of it. Many companies go under from misreading how much sufficient working capital they must have. There are different approaches to working this out (no pun intended).

Related a bit more to strategy, I will try and illustrate another situation in which capital is managed. Company x uses budgeting capital through its annual capital planning process (CPP). Capital expenditures, or capex, are assigned through the CPP. Management and the projects group then allocate and initiate the release of these capex monies. However, during the implementation of these projects, the expected accrued value generated from these expenditures are not fully tracked and recorded by the company's finance team.

Even though significant tangible business value is being generated in the form of new assets or to improve existing ones, the allocation of capex monies is only listed as a liability on the general ledger. It's not the management accountant's fault for this oversight. They have not received the accrued figures from the project management teams. From governance perspective there is no process to monitor and record this value within the organisation.

In this scenario capital is only an expenditure line item even though it's meant as investment money to grow the business. An organisation spends a little to gain additional value in the process. I'm continually surprised by how so few people think about the capital life cycle – its intended value and scope within the organisation. Yet it is capital that makes a business go and grow.

Some of the reasons for this oversight most likely originate from the narrow definitions of what constitutes business value. In a world where greater social demands are being asked of businesses, how can a business describe its tangible value back to a community or its customers? The narrow definitions of value do not give accountants the latitude they need to reflect this type of business value.

I passionately believe there's a strong need to better understand and classify the various forms of business value. Only then can value be matched to an applicable form of capital beyond what is today recorded on accounting statements.

The business benefits are immeasurable. Strategic intent becomes a strategic mandate. Strategic plans for the first time have full traceability back to the board and shareholders. It forges a stronger bond between management accountants, marketing and business strategists who each independently wrestle with business growth challenges every day. Tangible strategic outcomes could now be appropriately measured on a company's bottom line. As any good strategist is often aware, follow the money trail to find the source of pain.

Additionally, an organisation can immediately be more profitable by unlocking existing business value that has been perpetually trapped within it. Better classifying value will better define the nature of the organisation; to include the social value it already generates. These combined benefits position an organisation for a significant competitive edge.

I believe there are three essential capital buckets at an organisation's disposal: a) financial, b) investment, and c) social. These each can be described as a particular organisation barometer.

- ***Financial** Capital = Wealth **Distribution***
- ***Investment** Capital = Wealth **Creation***
- ***Social** Capital = Wealth **Enablement***

Financial Capital is already mature and being practiced by every organisation. I define it here as the means to financially improve the company by using accounting approaches such as tax minimisation strategies, entity structuring, transfer pricing, re-invoicing (an off shoring approach) and other financial instruments. Each are designed as a profit allocation method to bolster the financial position of the company to its shareholders and trustees.

During the past several decades for many mid to large-sized businesses, financial capital has been a driving force to increasing their profitability. Demonstrating healthy profit margins can in return allow organisations to seek and acquire additional funding to further grow and remain competitive.

That said securing additional funding is a positive by-product of financial capital, not its primary driver. Financial capital's primary value is to redistribute existing wealth rather than directly contribute to the creation of new wealth.

By re-distributing capital it shifts the balance of who stands to benefit and who doesn't. Those that benefit the most not only gain greater wealth but also increased influence and higher political clout. From a business context this can be advantageous to the longevity of a company and its brand.

The importance in financial capital over the past two or three decades can be demonstrated in the correlation to less rigid financial regulatory regimes. This in turn has fuelled the popular rise of ever more ingenious financial channels and instruments to take advantage of deregulated markets. Obviously the global financial crisis is a recent case in point.

I will always remember the first minutes of my MBA accounting class when the instructor famously said 'I am not here to teach you science, but instead to teach you art.' There are a host of recently published books describing financial capital in greater detail such as *Treasure Islands* by Nicholas Shaxson.

Perhaps lost in all this fanciful financial gamesmanship is the real reason organisations exist. To build value that guarantees both the business and its customers mutually benefit.

Investment capital is about acquiring strategic assets as a result of, or to provide, greater growth opportunities. This form of capital is the primary growth engine of the organisation, or wealth creator. If strategically planned, delivered and managed well, these new operational assets fuel company growth.

This growth subsequently adds more employment opportunities. For those brick and mortar businesses these employment opportunities are nearby communities impacted by an organisation's physical presence.

Investment capital not only strengthens and anchors the company's bedrock, but also returns positive economic gains to the communities closest to company's physical locations. Growth of course does not necessarily translate to profitability. Profitability is a positive by-product of investment capital, but not its main driver.

Strategies around asset acquisition and delivery are central to the success of investment capital. Traditionally this has been the domain of capital planning processes and project delivery.

As described earlier in the book often times investment capital is allocated on the principle of 'he who shouts loudest' wins the allocated monies. Therefore, investment capital is often times applied to more operational efficiency-styled purposes. In another words, much of the capital invested does not go to actual strategic growth initiatives.

It is difficult to unlock business value in an organisation driven by operational efficiencies. Everyone is doing their own thing with blinders on, so why would they care? The wealth enablement parameters need to be reset to challenge the status quo of why they *should* care.

Social capital has come a long way in the past decade, gaining international acceptance. I choose here to loosely define it as the investment of people and communities impacted by a business's activities. This not only includes those not directly affiliated with the organisation, it also includes those who work for the organisation as well.

In essence it is part public value (external value) and part employee entitlement within places of work (internal value). To measure external value, this type of capital requires business government partnership to agree to the form of value delivered. Internal value can come from various new approaches to measuring the human condition within organisations. As explored in several previous chapters, social capital can indeed be measured.

Without a workforce, organisations would cease to exist. Without communities of customers who choose to transact with organisations, again organisations would cease to exist. Think of social capital as the 'enablement of wealth'. Wealth cannot be created or re-distributed without social capital to tap into.

A highly skilled workforce, a result from repeated social and investment capital inputs, generates competitive advantages. Together these two forms of capital not only raise the standard of living in communities, additional capital infusion also attracts a higher talent pool of workers who in turn marshal new business innovation. The cycle repeats itself, something akin to a positive 360-degree feedback loop. One only has to think of Silicon Valley or an established research hub like the Boston area to demonstrate this symbiotic relationship.

By a company investing wisely in its people and the communities most impacted, the ability to grow its business dramatically increases. So does its ability to increase its profitability, attracting even more investment and social capital. Well-invested social capital can enable happy, content and well-off communities who are fully involved and engaged in their work environments.

Those reading may be curious as to why I left out the value of private equity. After all private equity is a large generator of capital in many parts of the western world.

PE, as it is commonly referred to, largely depends on the particular release terms of capital into an organisation. PE commonly has attributes of both investment and financial capital.

The capital is usually raised from retail and institutional investors to provide value such as funding new emerging technologies, expanding existing investment capital, performing acquisitions, or to simply strengthen a balance sheet. As PE is quite a flexible model and a popular way to raise capital, I tend to think of it more like a funding channel rather than a fixed, capital bucket.

To better illustrate the value of these three forms of capital, they can be aligned to the OrgPi model introduced in the last chapter.

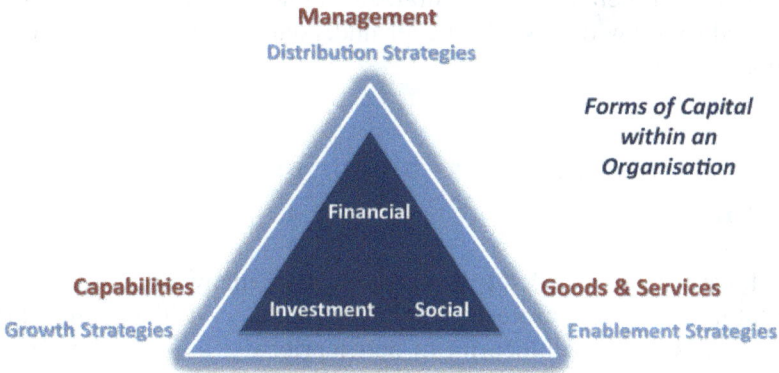

Financial capital is primarily about profitability. The primary job of management is to ensure the financial stability of the organisation. To grow a business requires investment capital to strengthen its internal set of capabilities. Finally maintaining the delivery of a high quality of goods and services requires a strong and supportive workforce and positive relationships with customers and affected communities.

The new art of business strategy actually emphasizes the last two forms of capital – investment and social. Rediscovering business strategy is in some ways about rediscovering our capitalistic roots; a return to investment and societal basics to recapture our society's wealth generation engine. It speaks to the tagline, 'profit with purpose'.

Who in the organisation is most fit to lead this new way of strategising, and what of the management accountant role? Are management accountants, trained and versed in the value of financial capital, good stewards in managing the use of investment and social capital? Would your organisation put its innovation strategy in the hands of management accountants?

This is not to say that financial experts should be absent from strategic discussions. It is instead suggesting financial leaders shouldn't be the sole inputs to achieving business growth. Their traditional influence at the strategic table should be somewhat balanced to allow others who better understand investment and social capital an equal voice.

The power of a business blueprint for capital planning

I earlier described the shortcomings in many organisations to allocating capital for project planning purposes. I'd like to introduce the use of a business blueprint to better prioritise allocation of capex monies.

As mentioned in the chapter, 'What are the Strategic Boundaries?' there is no single definition of strategic management that can adequately capture what it is. Instead it's more akin to a concept that is a sum of two essential parts – strategic thinking and strategic enablement. A business blueprint, designed well, can be the missing link between these two concepts illustrated below.

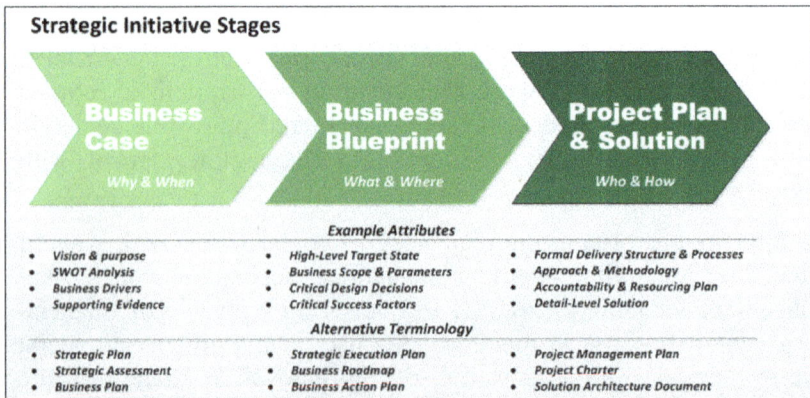

Strategic Initiative Stages

Business Case	Business Blueprint	Project Plan & Solution
Why & When	What & Where	Who & How

Example Attributes

• Vision & purpose	• High-Level Target State	• Formal Delivery Structure & Processes
• SWOT Analysis	• Business Scope & Parameters	• Approach & Methodology
• Business Drivers	• Critical Design Decisions	• Accountability & Resourcing Plan
• Supporting Evidence	• Critical Success Factors	• Detail-Level Solution

Alternative Terminology

• Strategic Plan	• Strategic Execution Plan	• Project Management Plan
• Strategic Assessment	• Business Roadmap	• Project Charter
• Business Plan	• Business Action Plan	• Solution Architecture Document

This planning lifecycle diagram is a framework meant to highlight and guide the planning process to a better set of rationalised decisions. Depending on an organisation's governance maturity, some may choose to combine the Business Blueprint stage with the Business Case stage, whilst others may split the Project Plan from the Solution process.

Where would financial controls fit into this framework? Depending on governance controls in place, the Business Case or Business Blueprint stages could allocate an initial high-level estimate that would include indicative costs. It is not until the Project Plan & Solution stage where detail costing would be provided. If the project plan is approved, the allocated funds are adjusted downward accordingly and formally approved for use.

If there was one theme or pattern I experienced in my professional career it was not enough time and effort went into analysing the what and where side of planning. Often times these important questions were skipped over for expediency purposes. It was these questions that later came back to haunt projects in the form of as scope variance (which translated to budget overruns and delays).

The business blueprint stage works in form and function much like a house blueprint. The blueprint describes what the house will look like and exactly where it belongs from a foundational point of view.

It addresses the needs and wants of the homeowner much like a business case would. The needs and wants of a family are quite diverse such as house aesthetics, usefulness of the surrounding land, the design theme, building longevity, and any unique building material that could disrupt the design. An architect needs to consider all these things when providing a high level design.

By adopting the use of a business blueprint, the organisation has a foundation in which to build future business value. The business can also return to this blueprint to help control any future project variances that may present themselves. If variances are accepted, this blueprint can identify and measure those business gaps between the blueprint and the variance.

Having this knowledge can ensure organisational change remains front and centre within the organisation, that change itself is not too disruptive. The blueprint can help tease out the nature of this disruption to keep expectations in check.

When presented for the first time with the concept of a business blueprint, it can be confronting to many stakeholders. Senior managers may struggle with this new design oriented deliverable, especially if they have not used modelling in their own business domains. Questions like, 'why do we need something different than what other projects do?' and 'why are we being treated differently?' have been questions I have heard often.

I suppose it's a natural fear of the unknown and it may take some extra time to win them over. However once people begin to realise the numerous benefits, and how similar in value it is to a house blueprint, many become very appreciative of this 'extra step'.

This rings especially true for those program or project managers who realise that many of their delivery risks have just been qualified and measured. It is one less thing for them to worry about. If there are any future design issues, they simply call on the project architect next time as opposed to working through design-related aspects themselves.

Co-dependencies, marketing versus technology

The Internet boom period (often referred to as the Dot Com Bubble) came to a dramatic end through the NASDAQ trading market. That market, trading heavy in tech stocks, lost 10% of its entire value in a single day in March 2000. Many were in denial that day, over exuberance perhaps, but for others it was the signal marking the beginning of the end to an incredible technology run.

It took about another year to conclude that the tech bubble had indeed burst. Those who still held technology shares had accepted they would not see their stock prices return to those lofty levels again. It was a permanent market correction to the value of technology.

The correction had a rippling effect in the way business perceived their IT departments. No longer were IT departments viewed as special with their own research and development budgets to control. Many businesses started to view their IT departments simply as a service provider of technology.

This meant greater financial control and rigour was needed, much like any other service group such as Human Resources and Marketing. It became commonplace to have a Chief Information Officer (CIO) report into the Chief Financial Officer instead of the CEO to ensure what IT spent was not only known but also accounted for.

In response to these significant changes many IT departments started to centralise their operations. The new subject domains of architecture and IT governance became tools to meet this new reporting and management frontier.

A large portion of most IT operations was spent on back-office corporate centralisation activities. This work is often complex, requiring heavy investment to connect key business systems that are essential to running a business.

This was still a period where much of the world continued to practice 'Kaizen' as the preferred form of staying competitive. Back-office centralisation served as an important pillar to this competitive world. As the business world became ever more interconnected, more was demanded of IT departments to make it a reality. Complexity continued to increase and costs continue to rise.

Something had to give, and it did. First a wave of IT outsourcing then followed by a wave of cheaper Cloud hosting models, crashed over every IT department. Senior executives were challenging IT departments to find further cuts or be made redundant.

Yet what happened next has significantly changed the role of technology once again. Technology value up to this point in time was always being pushed out by businesses to their customers. The slogans are familiar with many of us, 'try our new website' or 'check out our latest electronic product'.

To be sure, businesses had the customer in mind when they designed their sites and products. Yet these examples illustrate a time when businesses were assuming what customers preferred without much direct customer feedback.

With the advent of a consumer-driven business world, no longer does this logic apply. The inverse is now happening as consumers begin dictating the technology terms.

As an example when I worked for a transportation agency in the late 2000s, a young and switched-on developer put together a mobile app that allowed the public to see our transportation timetable on their phones. It also reported how late the next service was.

How did he manage to do this on his own without any assistance from my organisation? He simply downloaded the necessary public data and built his own app. His app even made the papers, which tarnished our organisation in the process. Naturally our IT department was put into emergency mode. We had to stop what we were working on to immediately reorient our work into developing our own mobile timetable app to defend our competency. That's the power of the consumer who knows technology and can weld direct influence to changing a business's investment priority!

Businesses need to act on customer technology expectations in ways never before envisioned. Roundtable discussions are now about innovation instead of the latest process efficiency. Phrases like 'our customers are telling us that they want a mobile app to do x', and 'do we have the right data to tell us we are adequately listening to our customers in order to maintain their loyalty?' These questions are replacing scenarios such as 'business group x wanting to purchase software y to make them more efficient'.

These business groups are under pressure to deliver and are searching for technology-minded people who can help them. Do they turn to the IT shop, perhaps a vendor who has a cool application in the Cloud, or do they look to hire in technical resources of their own? Leadership has to think twice whether it truly wants to outsource its entire IT department.

These new consumer-driven expectations also extend out to the marketing group. The result has seen marketing departments given larger budgets to help understand their customers better.

No longer is procuring new technology investments exclusively a CIO role. Increasingly a Chief Marketing Officer (CMO) is given access to and command of an innovation budget as their strategic value increases. Given this it's little wonder the marketing department is becoming more tech-savvy than ever before.

To achieve their aims many marketing departments have identified two critical success factors, or CSFs. One is ensuring their employees, as organisational champions, embrace the digital world (if they haven't already). The second CSF is obtaining additional technology investment to deliver those digital aims. These two CSFs allow marketing to make better use of consumer-based information, whilst at the same time harnessing new technology investments, like social media and ever-innovative marketing campaigns.

The IT and Marketing departments have in practice been edging closer together – each requiring the other to add more credence to their value. Both the CIO and CMO are becoming more aligned to each other's wants and needs.

If technology can be effectively harnessed by the CMO, then the organisation increases the chances to become more competitive. From an IT department perspective, these departments have collected an immense amount of business knowledge within the organisation; vital for a marketing department thirsting for quality information. Furthermore, IT architects are perfectly placed to spot business gaps and inefficiencies and offer potential solutions. Their own knowledge provides invaluable strategic insights for the CMO and their staff.

An example of potential collaboration is search engine marketing, or SEM. SEM is the application of online marketing strategies to ensure greater online visibility of one's business by producing better search engine results. Better results in turn can lead to higher sales volume.

Today nearly every online business is running its own SEM campaigns. This means there is additional competition and as a result, malicious Internet tactics are on the rise. Terms like 'hide and seek attacks' and 'hit inflation' are techniques competitors can use to unfairly distort a business's online presence. These tactics can reduce customer traffic to a business site. Less traffic means less sales. One study described an advertiser scenario this way:

> *Some advertisers perform hit inflation attacks on competitor advertisers. Such advertisers employ techniques that would continuously visit Web sites where they expect to find their competitors' advertisements and click on the displayed advertisement if it belongs to one of their competitors. Although this does not directly generate revenue to the fraudulent advertiser, it depletes the advertising budgets of its competitors, and hence limits the exposure of its competitors to the market (Metwally, Agrawal and Abbadi 2006, 4).*

There's a good likelihood for increased coordinated Internet attacks and industrial digital sabotage. It's one thing to put into place a competitive online strategy, yet another to maintain that position. An Internet marketing strategy's execution will need to consider how best to do this. The strategy will require input from both IT and Marketing departments.

In a way the success of online sales is being driven by what both IT and Marketing departments do (or don't do). This is a new frontier where sales departments are increasingly interconnected to other business groups

Working together, architects and marketing strategists are a powerful combination within any organisation. Jamie Barnett, a CMO with Netskope, summed the relationship up this way:

> *"As I look for business value in the technology itself, my CIO increasingly becomes my strategic partner and advisor… I need him to help me think through my goals and potential issues I may not be considering, such as how secure the apps are that my team is using, what happens when a disaster or technology failure*

*occurs, whether we are properly safeguarding our customers'
data, and whether we're getting the most out of the systems we're
using (Lazauskas 2014)."*

Here are some additional reasons I'd like to add:

- *Study any IT and Marketing job postings and you'll likely come across the need for a CDO, Chief Digital Officer; it's a new executive-level position that straddles these two worlds.*

- *The same is true for another executive-level position, the CCO or Chief Customer Officer.*

- *That there are two new C-level roles (CDO and CCO) suggests industry recognition for the unique value between customer, marketing and technology.*

- *There are more CMO seats at the executive table, demonstrating the added influence they now carry.*

- *A large organisation I recently worked for centralised their marketing departments to deliver higher customer value and brand recognition.*

The alternative to not working together is something short of an internal war for political clout and budgetary control. It can start with marketing wanting to innovate but not wanting to have to cut through IT red tape (as they may see it). Conversely IT leadership prefers to have Marketing follow its policies and not talk to vendors it is unaware of (Lazauskas 2014).

I mention the more problematic issues as walls can be easily put up yet are harder to tear down. Hardly the type of situation an organisation wants as it transitions itself to become more customer focused.

To improve the divide between these two senior roles, the traditional role of the CIO reporting into the CFO should be given a second look. Each organisation is naturally different. As technology becomes ever more pervasive, the role of IT departments need greater scrutiny beyond a budgetary point-of-view.

IT departments should not be everything to everyone. It's just not practical, nor feasible, in today's working landscape. Discovering what an IT department does well and doesn't do well is a long-overdue organisational exercise.

The value of a semi-permanent business change group

There are repeated failures on multiple levels with executing strategy. It's the Achilles Heel of strategic management practices. Though the reasons are numerous two stand out: lack of adequate scope planning, and failure to consistently communicate across the organisation during the strategic delivery.

Both reasons have a common theme – the existing business groups responsible for planning and communications are overrun by the sheer complexity and added pressures in performing strategic change. Everyone has his or her day job and it usually does not include strategic management.

How many situations honestly exist where a large group of operational resources had to drop what they were doing to help the organisation plan, prepare and execute the organisation's strategy? What organisational planners factor in shuffling of resources into and out of a strategic initiative, as well as ensure what that change of roles will mean to those resources and their operational units? These answers are either ignored or forgotten in most planning exercises.

More likely than not those affected resources are given some latitude in their schedules to assist the strategic initiative, but are still required to perform their other duties as well. The result is that many of these individuals find it difficult to cope with two competing roles. As I covered earlier it's quite a leap for managers to transition to directors, yet that is what is temporarily asked of these resources.

Many simply cannot cope and those that can usually work longer hours to juggle both roles. Stress levels inevitably increase as no one wants to perform dual roles, especially if there is no reward or incentive attached. An increase in stress levels also decreases the objectivity in performing strategic management activities. Emotions dictate the pace and the result often erodes the potential value of the intended change.

Unfortunately, there is no single 'how-to' book or best practice for strategic execution. Even if one organisation is nearly identical to another, it does not guarantee that each of these organisations should copy each other in performing business change. Each has its own cultural norms and different business practices that create uniqueness.

One organisation I knew was going through not only a significant internal consolidation, it was during a period of industry compliance reforms that were the largest in some fifty years. In essence the organisation experienced significant change on top of significant change!

There is an alternative planning approach to lessen the burden of change to the workforce and management. Setting up a formalised but temporary business change program can reduce operational disruptive risk.

The concept of a business change program, or BCP, is based on establishing an organisational management structure to exclusively transform a large part of the organisation to another operational state. This structure is temporary, serving only for a period of time during the transformation, which is usually three to five years.

By facilitating change to better ensure its success, the BCP works like an organisational pressure valve, taking pressure and stress away from operations having to manage the change. A BCP is not a program of works being managed from existing management structures like a program management office. Instead it is a new 'semi-permanent' structure with its own line of management accountabilities. It should require board approval – more on that later.

A large multi-billion dollar organisation I know well has been going through a massive change program across much of their organisation. The 5-year program vision is meant to fundamentally change the way the business operates to make it more customer-focused. A semi-permanent management structure was setup to orchestrate and manage the various business unit change initiatives.

There is no single existing business group responsible for the change management authority. The program is simply too large. It would smother the existing program office and its resources (which have other accountabilities already assigned to that business group). The program's reach impacts so many business groups in different ways the organisation requires something unique to manage the change.

Yet another example is a large financial institution in Australia. Last decade it initiated a long-standing cultural transformation program called 'Breakout'. By 2006 when it had already run for six years, some 26,000 employees had participated in Breakout workshops.

The aim of the program was to create "a high performance, value-driven organisation that is delivering real competitive advantage that benefits all of its stakeholders (ANZ Bank n.d., 11)." The bank recognised that its transformation was a journey, not a one-off exercise.

The results speak for themselves. In the first 5 years the share price grew over 60%, market capitalisation doubled, and staff engagement also reached 60%, outstripping many large Oceania companies and outperforming the financial services benchmark of 51% (ANZ Bank n.d., 8-10).

A business change program can go by many different names such as Strategic Program Group or Transformation [insert name here] Standing Committee. Whatever the name, these instruments are useful in leading organisations through periods of major strategic transformation. They alone though cannot guarantee success.

A BCP obviously requires an authority higher than itself to ensure (as an escalation channel) the organisation can successfully move from A to B. Gaining C-level endorsement may not be enough appropriate authority. Most change programs are multiyear in duration.   It's likely one or more C-level positions will become vacated as new people rotate into these roles.

Often times with new blood comes a new mandate, or perhaps even a new direction.   Nothing can do more damage to a change initiative than the introduction of new leadership.   Though there will always be strategic issues to contend with, it's imperative to have leadership sustainability and authoritative continuity throughout a change initiative.   This is where the organisational board can fill a valuable role.

Many company boards operate under tight structures, roles and governance.   Many are therefore not well equipped to oversee a major change initiative.   An independent advisory board, on the other hand, can be established under the auspices of its board members.   Its sole purpose is to monitor the organisation's transformation journey, much the same way the BCP operates.   The BCP now has an escalation path should the need be warranted.

An advisory board monitoring a long-standing strategic initiative can act as a shield for the executive team, keeping them at arm's length from the usual politics of the board.   Ideally its membership should have expertise in performing strategic transformation initiatives.   This advisory board plays a crucial mediator-like role in bridging the expectation gap between both groups.

A major change initiative needs to be thought of as just that, a significant change to an organisation.   So why do companies continue to believe they can initiate change inside their organisation without changing it's thinking to perform that change?   It's a recipe for disaster.

A business change program has the freedom to put into place a way of initiating and monitoring change that operational groups simply cannot do.   For example, it can find the right balance between external consultants and seconded operational resources.   It can identify overlooked critical success factors to guide the transformation of the organisation.   Putting aside additional funds to create and operate a BCP can save significant dollars and a company's reputation in the process.

Rethinking those rusty and outdated organisational pipes

One of the biggest challenges to performing transformational change is replacing what I like to call 'rusty old pipes', or the organisational plumbing itself. Replacing these outdated pipes is arguably the hardest thing to do within an organisation. Replace these and organisations can truly reinvent themselves.

Rusty pipes are the old and stale vertical management lines of reporting to include the antiquated governance decision-making apparatuses that support these reporting lines. These pipes are unfortunately now working against the effectiveness of organisations.

Some reading this may be thinking I have gone a bit mad this time. Changing a culture and introducing new technologies surely doesn't mean tampering with structures that are time tested.

Every good thing comes to an eventual end. These pipes have more or less been around since the last iteration of the industrial revolution in the early part of the 20th century. That's a very long time.

They are an antiquated management structure based on defined roles and on command and control decision-making. I'm not arguing that this structure no longer has any merit – far from it. These pipes we take for granted are under enormous strain in today's ever-quickening pace of decision-making, continuous change and automation.

In particular, automation today is more about cross-functional automation and less about automation within a particular business silo. It is cutting horizontally across many of these old rusty pipes, placing additional strain on them.

Imagine a decades-old dock built on a set of metal pylons. There's a river (representing automation) flowing through these pylons (representing slow, vertical decision-making). The water not only makes the pylons rust over time, but in return the pylons prevent the water from flowing in a more natural and efficient way.

To continue the analogy, many pylons have small rust holes in them where water is seeping through. Historically, decision-making has been focused on patching these holes rather than considering the future state of the pylons.

Over the years the river has grown wider and deeper. No one in upper management, who are high up on the dock, can see what is happening at the water level to consider ways of replacing the damaged pylons. The strength of the water flow has gradually increased over the years so as to not alarm management, especially as many in management have not been around to see the gradual changes in the river. From where management sit there appears to be little rust and the water seems to be flowing at a reasonable pace.

To demonstrate this from a realistic scenario, I'll examine a stereotypical role at a stereotypical office environment in Normalville, insert-country-name-here. The person in question is John Smith (of course) and he manages invoice processing within the finance department.

John spends much of his day processing a range of corporate invoices. He uses a software system that allows him to automate much of his tasks. The system is also linked to other departments, such as purchasing, with many work tasks being mapped to an automated workflow environment.

John's primary objective is not how many invoices he can process (the system largely does that) instead his role is more about quality assurance (QA). He approves invoice exceptions. He needs to review each exception on a case-by-case basis to determine whether the invoice can be approved.

This may sound trivial but invoice exceptions have become a major problem for many large organisations. The Spend Matter's website reported that "roughly 1 in 3 invoices tied to a PO (purchase order) requires manual touch points before approval to pay (Busch 2013)". John's organisation is not far off that average, so that is potentially a lot of work to perform.

John may need to interact with a number of people before he passes judgment about a particular exception. An individual he talks with could include the invoice requester, John's account payables manager and someone from purchasing. He may also need to manually adjust a value in the invoice system. Depending on his level of authority, he may need to talk to the system administrator to gain authorisation to make a change from time to time.

In another words, he spends much of his time on the phone and in email, chasing other people. His job function is considered critical to making sure all invoices are transacted as well as possible. The organisation would rather not outsource this QA role.

As life would have it for John, the company is under constant change, especially when restructures are announced. There are also continual system tweaks and policy changes to the invoicing administrative rules. These events when they occur tend to create more invoice exceptions than the normal load expected. It all adds up to keeping John quite busy.

Can you catch where this is going? Critical as his role is, the invoice processing function involves more stakeholders than just him. It encompasses John's accounts payable manager, system administrators, the requestors and at times procurement for contract management guidance.

Though technology advances have created plenty of back-office automation between different business groups, many of the pre-automation roles from the past have not changed that much today. This actually creates more governance than necessary. (The water flow has widened and increased with intensity to affect more of the organisation.)

The traditional accountability rules do not take full advantage of technology value being introduced. In many organisations our working lives have been made more complex by creating technological automation whilst preserving our old decision-making structures.

Imagine a world where John is not only his own manager, he is also part system administrator and part contract manager. In another words, John is responsible not only for the invoice processing function but also for the purchase to pay (P2P) lifecycle where certain named accounts are concerned.

And John would not be the only person to have such an independent authority. There may be other John-like people responsible for other type of accounts. Why would this be better?

John's accountability is clearly defined and measured. He doesn't need to rely on others to perform well, and he need not point a finger in defence of his actions. He is responsible for managing the entire lifecycle of that invoice. The full suite of responsibilities is now better aligned to the promises the invoice management technology was meant to deliver.

John's performance can now sky rocket. His time management no longer requires chasing and notifying people of his actions. Best of all, John is empowered to own more of the business function, doing it more efficiently than what it took three people to once perform.

His confidence soars and he feels more satisfied with his work. He no longer goes home each night feeling frustrated about how he struggled to convince his boss to grant an exception even though enough adequate evidence was presented. He no longer is asked to patch holes in rusted pylons. He operates from a new floatable dock where management is just around the corner for any support he may need.

The story of John is not unique. It is found in nearly every business unit somewhere.

It's about creating new organisational mechanisms to align governance across horizontal business functions rather than roles designed around vertical management decision-making. Employees are measured against these additional responsibilities. No longer is the organisation straddled by accountability confusion.

Best of all these new mechanisms eventually remove the need for business silos by reducing single points of operational failure. John no longer represents the lone invoice processing QA guy everyone is waiting on. If John takes work leave, another similar person performing the same activities elsewhere simply steps in to assume his position.

There is no need to temporarily train someone for his role, as it is no longer specialised and unique. The invoicing function increases capability performance whilst enabling better employee performance.

In a worst case scenario say John unfortunately makes a few poor approval decisions. The financial performance efficiencies gained by removing his QA specialist role and replacing it with a more encompassing role will more than offset the financial misjudgements from approving a few poor invoice exceptions. Besides, the software system can be better tuned to ensure the worst case scenarios are minimised.

John's scenario is actually quite conservative. In past organisations I have been involved with, there are multiple levels of invoice approval. I have seen upwards of four levels (of people like John), and in one organisation I recently heard there were a chart-topping eleven levels of invoice approval gates! Imagine the red tape and inefficiencies that exist in that organisation.

In a world of constant change companies who allow their workforce to perform multiple cross-functional activities, stand to best benefit. Here are some summarised reasons:

- *A single resource is easier to identify and chase for a particular business issue than chasing many.*

- *Employees are generally happier about their work as they gain a deeper sense of ownership.*

- *Multi-functional employees have a higher likelihood of staying with the organisation as they seek their next work opportunity within the organisation instead of outside of it.*

- *By constantly rotating employees, they acquire ever more knowledge and skills, which in turn allows them to become better experts and champions for the business.*

- *Multi-functional opportunities engender empowering and positive feedback loops for both management and staff within the organisation*

Still not convinced? Look at the rise of IQ scores to see the type of world our society is marching towards. To my own amazement I learned there have been a number of studies repeatedly examining this fascinating area.

One such study, the 'Flynn Effect', drew the conclusion that "over the past 100 years, Americans' mean IQ has been on a slow but steady climb. Between 1900 and 2012, it rose nearly 30 points, which means that the average person of 2012 had a higher IQ than 95 percent of the population had in 1900 (Winerman 2013)."

I should add that these types of studies are not without controversy. Do they tell us that we are getting smarter and increasing our overall intelligence? Most academics argue this is simply too hard to prove from the studies.

That said the Flynn Effect does suggest a few things. Based on analysing the IQ results, people's cognitive problem solving skills and ability to mentally cope better in a more complex world, have both increased in score (Winerman 2013).

Assuming this to be true then we should be more adept at performing multiple activities. (This has nothing in common with multi-tasking.) Then why do businesses still insist on patching those rusty management pipes of the past? It not only demeans our intellectual capabilities as individuals, it also devalues our collective working contributions.

Numerous studies show workplace unhappiness levels at all-time highs. There is no reason why we shouldn't take back our confidence and self-esteem in our workplace. Let's move away from the disempowered, robotic, hypnotic, and mind numbing roles many people find themselves in today.

Why am I passionate about all of this? These rusty pipes are on the verge of collapsing, if they haven't already in some industries. I have counted myself as one of these unhappiness statistics at various times. I believe there is a better alternative that embraces higher company growth and prosperity.

Look again at technology to provide the impetus of change. Technology investments continue to slowly erode the old decision-making structures. Think of it as the salt in the earlier pylon-water flow analogy.

Peer into many technology departments and find some levels of staff rotation are already happening. For the past two decades IT staff continue to take on a wide range of diverse roles. It is not uncommon to hear the phrase, 'jack-of-all-trades' when fellow IT people describe what each other do.

Imagine if both IT and non-IT staff were rotated in and out of technology-based projects. Assuming 'technology is business and business is technology', then wouldn't this be a natural fit? Many non-IT employees already know quite a bit about technology, especially the younger generations moving into the workforce.

Each person would better appreciate what their business colleagues do and how technology is affecting their working lives. It might spark many ah-ha moments and perhaps unlock some innovative gems waiting to be discovered. Why shouldn't staff engagement models be designed around this concept?

Another option is to introduce one or more new C-level positions, such as the Chief Digital Officer or the Chief Customer Officer. Having a C-level role created, especially one that straddles the business and technology spaces, affords the organisation the ability to experiment with new management structures that are less specialised and more aligned to today's business challenges.

It all starts with replacing many of those rusty pipes. It should be the efficiency target that in turn will fuel the innovation engine for organisations.

The use of brokering services as a new approach

Perhaps a question is more appropriate to start with: What is a broker and a brokering service? There are numerous definitions but I'll suggest that a broker is someone who handles a transaction between two or more parties. Essentially a broker is a gun-for-hire to help represent, or protect, the client's best interests from a situation that is deemed quite complex and challenging for the client to work through on their own. It differs from a consultant in that a broker is fully representative of their client, whereas a consultant delivers a set of pre-negotiated services.

Originally intended for a financial arrangement, the term has also become popular within technology circles to describe someone who can act as a subject matter advisor when discussing a deal. An example might be providing assistance during a new Cloud services contract arrangement.

Finding a customer-centric strategist can be a difficult proposition for many businesses. Good talent is hard to come by, and there may be no qualified individual within the organisation. What should a business do in the meantime? They simply cannot wait to hire the best talent if they are planning their strategy.

Why not apply the same brokering principles to the strategic management frontier? Finding someone who can become embedded in the organisation for a period of time to represent the strategic management arm of the organisation (until such period that their services are no longer needed).

The use of a broker simplifies a range of diverse and complex challenges to leadership. Someone who presents well and can represent strategic trade-offs in an objective and non-partisan way.

The broker also makes an excellent sounding board to avoid planning road bumps along the way.

In another words the broker acts as a trusted, strategic partner. They ensure the ability to execute is not compromised or diminished. They serve in a similar way to a hired helmsman for a boat; tasked with steering the ship down a pre-ordained and navigable path.

This engagement model is markedly different to what a management consultant would perform. As earlier examined management consultancy firms are good at performing specific sets of tasks. Who performs them is largely left to the discretion of the firm. Its primary function is to match the best people to the most appropriate service it has at its disposal.

The company receiving the service must trust in the consultancy arrangement based on brand and reputation. There are generally no penalties or rewards for the final outcomes of that service.

Strategic thinking and strategic execution are two halves of a strategic canvas. Why would any CEO choose to outsource to a consultancy firm only half of its strategic equation? In this scenario (often performed around the world) the risks are all with the organisation *requesting* the consulting service. Only the brand and reputation are at risk for the consultancy firm. And depending on the situation, the damage done to a consulting service may be inconsequential as one unhappy customer amongst hundreds is not game changing stuff for the consultancy firm.

On the flip side if the strategy fails to deliver for the requesting organisation, it can seriously harm the future of that organisation. From a risk profile perspective this is quite an uneven playing field between two parties entering into a working relationship. Without a high level of trust between the parties, why would any leader seriously consider it?

At the end of the day it's easier to be strategic thinkers and much harder to own up to an execution plan and share in that accountability. With the risk profile lower, no wonder consultancy firms are all too willing to give advice when asked. It's also why a broker, acting as an independent and competent individual, is better placed to champion and work through the harder side of strategic execution.

In terms of structuring an appropriate broker package, there could be a flat fee plus a commission based on how successful the organisation was able to deliver against the strategic plan. The contract would need to address how any unforeseen events might affect the work, but much like a risk-reward contract structure, this one would pay out commissions when critical success factors were met.

Assuming a successful marriage occurs between a broker and their client organisation, there are a number of benefits for both.

The organisation:

- *... sees a more realistic strategic execution plan and significant reduction in its risk profile.*

- *... hand picks top strategic management talent without needing to trust a third party (consulting partner) to supply talent from their talent pool.*

- *... sets more manageable expectations with shareholders and its board.*

- *... has better awareness of the execution plan to include improved clarity around ownership and accountability.*

- *... can better communicate its strategic execution plan, which helps increase staff acceptance and participation levels.*

The broker:

- *... delivers better 'quality of service' value based on their deeper expertise, strengthening a trusted partner approach.*

- *... enters into an effective and flexible 'try-and-buy' engagement model retaining the option of contract renewal if job is performed well.*

- *... has financial incentive to perform to their level of expertise through a performance-based contract.*

Rediscovering the art of corporate social responsibility

Does anyone remember the previous incarnation called 'corporate responsibility' that swept the business world throughout the 1980s and early 90s? Today it might appear as just another fad or corporate gimmick of its day.

Well this time corporate social responsibility, commonly referred as CSR, may sound similar in name but there is something truly different. Unlike its earlier predecessor, this modified version of the original is reshaping both the value and underlying structure of businesses today.

When we think about social responsibility there is something inherently noble about wanting to save our planet, or simply being more charitable. These desires transcend into the organisations we work for.

Some organisations act upon our desires better than others. In the chapter about our human condition, this concept was explored as a 'conscious business' movement; a movement with the aim to address these new societal and individual desires through better management of corporate profits.

Take for example the often-cited Paul Newman line of salad dressings. Profits from the sales go back to charitable causes. In another words, the more profitable his products are, the more society benefits. In the 1990s when Paul Newman adopted this approach, it was considered quite innovative.

So successful was his model it has been repeated by many social-conscious businesses. One such business is Toms, an online shoe retailer that launched in 2006. Their business model is called 'one-for-one', matching every pair of shoes they sell with a pair of new shoes donated to a child in need. Over 35 million pairs of shoes have been donated. In fact, the program was so successful it expanded to include other initiatives such as an eyewear range that contributes to sight restoration for the vision impaired.

Study after study shows consumers would rather spend their hard earned income on a business if they think it is giving back to communities or causes they believe in; and consumers will still spend even if the product or service is higher priced.

In fact so many businesses are taking a similar path that a host of movements and corporate support structures are sprouting up around the world. A few are worth mentioning.

Perhaps the earliest attempt to recognise this new type of social business model is the not-for-profit organisation, Social Venture Network. Started in 1987, businesses that are or have been members include notable consumer brands such as Ben and Jerry's, The Body Shop, Birkenstock and Clif Bar.

A more recent initiative is called 'B Corp'. A 'beneficial' certification of authenticity to a commercial organisation that demonstrates providing high social value. The group that administers these certificates is called B Lab, a US not-for-profit organisation. They have worked to get a significant number of US States to pass legislation to adopt a new corporate entity status in support of these new B Corps. The difference between a B Corporation from a traditional business is in the way a company's financial performance is judged in providing social value.

B Corporation is also a group with a global reach. As of late May 2015 their website listed nearly 1,300 certified B Corps across 121 industries in 41 countries.

Another worth mentioning is 'Plan B' (also referred to as the 'B Team'). An initiative co-founded by Sir Richard Branson and Jochen Zeitz. The not-for-profit's mission and promise statement from their website is as follows:

> *"To catalyse a better way of doing business for the wellbeing of people and the planet... The private sector can and must redefine both its responsibilities and its own terms of success; a Plan B for concerted, positive action that will ensure business becomes a driving force for social, environmental and economic benefit."*

These examples demonstrate a growing movement to create new business endowment based on alternative operating principles. These principles guide the way in which businesses report the financial benefits they provide. Socially conscious consumers can now easily identify these organisations. They may wish to transact business with them, or perhaps choose to become investors. As is often said, it is truly a win-win proposition for both consumers and businesses.

Yet are these organisations truly successful? The book *Firms of Endearment* written by Raj Sisodia, David B Wolfe and Jag Sheth, analyses a number of companies practicing this approach and the business performance numbers are quite startling.

US-based companies outperformed the S&P 500 by 14 times over the course of 15 years. International companies outperformed by 10 times over the same period (see diagram below). With astronomical numbers such as this, it would be remiss to not explore the virtues of corporate social responsibility.

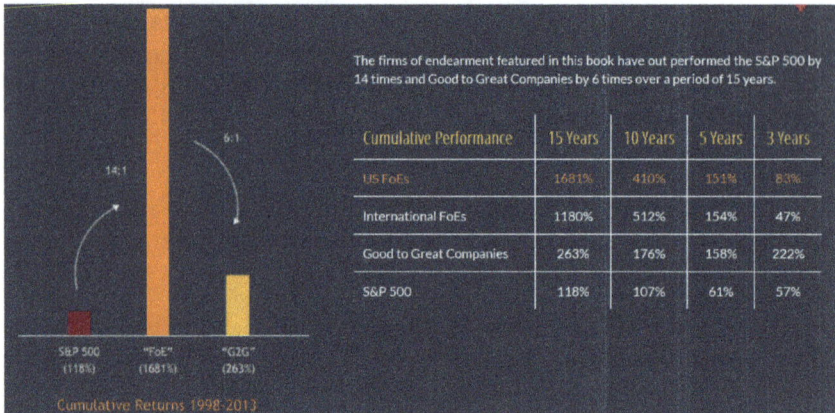

The firms of endearment featured in this book have out performed the S&P 500 by 14 times and Good to Great Companies by 6 times over a period of 15 years.

Cumulative Performance	15 Years	10 Years	5 Years	3 Years
US FoEs	1681%	410%	151%	83%
International FoEs	1180%	512%	154%	47%
Good to Great Companies	263%	176%	158%	222%
S&P 500	118%	107%	61%	57%

Cumulative Returns 1998-2013

(http://www.firmsofendearment.com/)

It's not just businesses that are becoming more socially conscious. Respected former world leaders have joined forces to push for a more humane and social-conscious world by setting up their own 'socially-conscious business club' called 'The Elders'.

Those that pursue this new approach to doing business stand to considerably gain not only in their sense of fulfilment of societal contribution, but also reputation and financial reward. Perhaps the early gimmick of the 1980s was nothing more than a false start?

Mimicking entrepreneurs to become innovative

Innovation is harder than it appears for companies who are large and in mature markets. The larger the business the higher number of business silos and planning complexity that potentially exists. The freedom to innovate becomes inversely proportional to the size of the business. In the words of Rowan Gibson, a best-selling author and leading expert on enterprise innovation:

> *"... innovation goes so much against the grain in most companies. It has to fight against a whole set of management principles, processes and systems that are basically set up to deliver something else (Gibson 2013)."*

An organisation does not have to be significantly large to find it difficult to innovate. Any organisation that adheres to regimented hierarchical management practices can also stymie innovation. Hierarchical performance models reinforce individual achievement at the expense of what might be best for the organisation.

An example includes the fear that a manager may steal a good idea from a subordinate. Another example is when an individual hoards their data (such as in Excel spreadsheets) to protect their knowledge. It might justify their influence and job security but it keeps a lid on good ideas from being properly assessed and tested.

We all know of a situation where someone who has been in a role for many years all of sudden quits or decides to retire. They were performing a critical job function. The organisation is caught unawares and scrambles to capture the intellectual capital (IC) that person has accumulated. The organisation's reaction and ability to capture that IC is futile at best. I even know cases where the organisation isn't even aware of that person's value and only learns of their contribution after their departure.

To reduce the hierarchical management impact on an organisation, creating an environment where there are frequent job rotations ensures business innovation does not die a quick death. The aim is to create a culture where employees are excited and enjoy new work opportunities. No one ever stays in a particular business function for too long.

Employees get cross-trained, always learning about a new part of the business. This increases job satisfaction levels and overall IC by reducing single resourcing points of failure. In many cases training an existing employee for a new role is cheaper than having to replace that role with someone from outside of the organisation.

A successful job rotation program can initiate a culture shift to a more multi-disciplinary work force, increases job retention rates and encourages employees to identify improvements, gaps or duplications within their organisation. It's an operational environment ripe for being more innovative.

In some ways creating a multi-disciplinary work force is not too different from creating an army of entrepreneurs. Entrepreneurs usually start with a particular idea or people talent they wish to bring to the market. Initially they lack other critical skills to achieving that aim. This might be in sales, marketing, product development or financial management for example. Through investor assistance or from their own merits, they become multi-skilled to take on the various business challenges that await them.

Creating an army of employees to think and act like an entrepreneur not only helps fuel new growth opportunities, it can also take the sting out of those corporate transformation programs. It injects fresh thinking and always challenges the status quo.

My own story as an entrepreneur has it origins at age 16 when I was a member of an entrepreneurial business club. My team and I set up a small venture to sell high-powered strobe lights for cars. They were the easiest things to assemble. It was part car headlamp and part rubber glove that fit around the lamp. The rubber glove contained a power adapter that was in the form of a cigarette lighter.

I honestly can't remember how many we made and sold but I do remember owning one that I used in my own car. They were extremely effective as an emergency and security power light. Our team was charged with tracking income, expenditures and marketing.

The experience gave me an early taste of how a small business operated. I graduated from this experience to launch my own widget-based business some two decades later by launching an innovative online music service in 2009.

I had initially created a music service for consumers who wanted to listen to their music collection online. Our tag line was 'Listen to the Internet in Stereo'. This service was launched before Yahoo, Google and others began offering their own subscription services. Once these global players entered the market I repositioned the service to solely focus on the commercial side.

Beyond a single account to manage and stream music, this new commercial service additionally offered an administrative service to control multiple accounts. This meant music-based partnering businesses could control the music played online for a range of other business affiliates.

Unlike the competitors of the day, I am proud to say that the business was the first global music service to be 100% Cloud-based when it was launched in 2009. When it was rebranded for the business community in 2012, the commercial administrative function was quite unique and different. From conception to closure, the business lasted about eight years during which time some $150k was invested into research and development.

There were many life lessons during those eight years. Perhaps the two most important (and relevant here) was the value of timing and visibility. I'm guessing many entrepreneurs can relate to both of these. Poor timing and lack of good visibility were significant contributors that led to closing its doors for business.

Related to timing, I was trying to raise capital at the exact time the Global Financial Crisis hit. Regrettably the crisis locked me out of cash liquidity from a private equity partner who was interested in sponsoring me. As a consequence, I not only lost an opportunity to raise significant funds, I also lost my 'hired gun' director positioned as part of a future private equity relationship.

Having someone of that calibre on my board would have gone a long way to increasing my business's visibility. Not to mention the value they would have brought to mentoring me. I had to go it alone financially if I wanted to continue pursuing my dreams.

I also didn't accurately predicate how long the music industry would continue its legal fights over copyright infringements. I assumed these legal battles would have been largely resolved before I launched my service. Instead they continued to drag on for several more years.

Though I was operating a legally safe business, even had several legal briefs prepared to back up those claims, my business was still impaired by the industry threats that were constantly in the papers. This greatly affected potential client and investor confidence.

I remember the countless people I met whose first question was about how my business stood up to the legal issues. It was definitely on everyone's mind at that time. Not only did I have to win people over about the viability of the business model, I also had to allay their fears from a legal point of view. Looking back, it was a tougher sell than I fully understood at the time.

By the time Yahoo and Google debuted their online music services, the legal battles did finally die down. I had to consider two options, exit out of the business because I couldn't compete with those global heavyweights, or begin reorienting it to a commercial model. In 2010 the commercial online music market was still very much immature.

It wasn't difficult to reorient the service. Much of the research and development was already completed. Besides I had put in significant funds and too much time into the business to simply throw in the towel. And I had developed a good relationship with a music business partner who shared the same commercial vision. It wasn't a hard decision to make.

Both of us set out to reorient and rebrand the service. By the time we were ready to pitch to our first customers, life had caught up to both of us. This is where a lack of visibility hurt the business.

With each holding down a full-time job neither of us could perform the necessary sales and marketing role the business demanded. Visibility requires a high amount of sales and marketing, especially for a small business we had.

If the business was to survive, we agreed that we needed to hire a business development specialist. This naturally would require more capital and we were already topped up. We would have to once again sell our model to potential investors; a proposition that once again would require a high amount of time and energy. We both came to the conclusion that perhaps it was time to sell it, and if that didn't work, simply shut it down. Though we momentarily had an interested buyer, the business ceased operating by the end of 2013.

My lessons learnt are in many ways the same when trying to create an innovative culture within an organisation. It too requires good visibility and timing. If business directors do not fully embrace the innovative initiative or are not even aware of its potential in helping to grow their business units, then all may be for naught.

One approach to reduce these twin risks is to adopt the use of innovation or entrepreneurial hubs. These hubs specialise in the capture and support of innovation happening within the organisation.

An innovation hub allows staff, low and middle management the opportunity to present their best innovative ideas and test them out in a controlled manner. It essentially gives a voice of support to the organisation's troops on the ground. The concept is similar to providing seed capital to an entrepreneur who has a good idea.

Here's a simple example of how it could work. An organisation chooses to set aside, or allocate, $200k into an annual innovation slush fund. Any qualified idea could receive up to $20k to test an idea in a controlled manner to determine if it meets expected business outcomes. This means the slush fund could accommodate up to ten ideas per year. If an idea meets or exceeds expected outcomes, it is subsequently rolled out to the wider organisation. Many angel investors would attest that it only takes one idea out of ten to recoup all the capital invested.

Some of these ideas may result in higher operational efficiencies, but the real innovative ideas could discover new distribution channels, new markets, products or pricing strategies that otherwise would have gone unnoticed by the management teams.

Innovation hubs need not be internally positioned within an organisation. External, or outsourced, hubs can perform much the same function.

An innovation hub negates the poor timing problem because it is a non-evasive extension of business-as-usual. Directors need not fear a disruptive change program affecting their operations. The hub is a 'light-touch' alternative.

The lack of visibility problem simply needs effective intra-company communications supported by a company-wide incentive program. A program tied to offering bonuses and appropriate recognition for cross-functional value creation.

It's worth mentioning that an innovation hub is quite different from a focus group formed to come up with new, innovative ideas. The use of focus groups is actually a common pitfall. Many studies have shown that putting smart people, or management, into a room does not create earth shattering new innovations.

Instead business innovation best happens in the field of practice. Ideas are born, and in some cases, tested by employees closest to where the action is. An organisation simply needs to provide the right support structure to see innovation come bubbling up to senior management. An innovation hub acts more as an enabler framework instead of a particular action plan that tries to answer, or solve discrete problems.

An example of an innovation hub changing both the culture and profitability of a large organisation is the Mexican global giant, CEMEX. Their $15b business from cement and building materials is now globally recognised for using alternative fuels to improving environmental performance. The company's phenomenal growth and global size came about from several tactical decisions to empower their work force.

Many of the new alternative fuel technologies were created from their SHIFT social platform. This platform allows their engineers and scientists to share success stories around their ready mix products. This sharing has increased the speed for product development to the market. Of significant internal importance, the platform has also been effective in identifying hidden talent within the organisation, thereby circumventing traditional hierarchical management systems (Skibola 2010). The platform's success has not only produced higher degrees of product innovation but has also retained and nurtured its internal talent in the process.

That is not the entire innovation success story. CEMEX management also scanned other industries outside of their own to discover new innovative approaches to doing business. They looked at the way FedEx and a few emergency services performed in-time logistics. The company then went about adopted similar approaches to transform its own order fulfilment processes (Cherry n.d.).

Sometimes industry change can come not from the trees but those that see the forest instead. We do not have to be experts in our field to necessarily see the value of what change can do.

I earlier mentioned my own online music business. I remain a devoted consumer of music, but never worked within the music industry. I, and other passionate consumers of music, saw the insatiable consumer demand for digital online music. Those of us who launched online music businesses wanted to participate in changing the face of an industry. In this case my business was not a success story but others were. Many gained serious attention and financial support by building new business models to better-fit consumer music experiences.

So how does an organisation tap into innovative talent sitting outside their organisation? External hubs, designed to be open and expressive innovation centres, can be a comfortable and engaging experience for outsiders to provide valuable feedback and insights.

Again outsiders need not be the smartest people in the room. They could be a collection of consumers taking part in a series of innovation sessions. Sometimes our harshest critics can become our most valuable champions if we look to these situations as opportunities rather than risk mitigation measures.

I end with a personal experience I'm reminded of when typing these words. It centres on my time spent living in Melbourne in the early noughties (early 2000s for those not in the know).

I had developed a friendship with someone who enjoyed talking politics as much as me. Though he and I viewed the world through two completely different lenses, we respected each other's abilities to debate in constructive ways. Each of us was a student of political history so we used our historical interpretations to back our opposing positions.

We had these engaging political conversations over coffee at a number of our favourite neighbourhood cafes. Back then we both had booming voices making it hard to whisper. (I must confess mine has become more tempered as age sets in.) So naturally patrons at the café could eavesdrop on us if they cared to listen.

I was gob smacked at how many wanted to join our discussion. A few even pulled their tables closer to us. As a comparison in the United States, where I come from, there may have been an altercation with others who did not agree and witnessed these open discussions on contentious issues in a public space.

Throughout these experiences two things never happened. We never saw anyone prematurely leave his or her table in protest. Secondly if they joined in the conversation, no one ever started an emotional tirade of their own while we all were discussing.

Years later I think about those unique encounters. The importance of what I was witnessing had nothing to do with politics, though it would have made for an interesting experiment. Instead, given the right situation people will and do engage if they see an opportunity to do so without risk of being confronted or abused.

Those who joined our conversations saw an opportunity to discuss a topic they were curious about. They saw an opportunity to do so in a manner that made them comfortable and which was non-threatening.

In a world where stress levels continue to rise, the constant bombardment of information overloads us, and our attention spans continue to shrink, the best ideas tend to come from situations of clarity, purpose and authenticity. My friend and I were living those moments in those Melbournian cafes.

I tend to believe as a society, we can truly accomplish more than we think possible. We only need to ensure the environment is conducive to innovative approaches.

CHAPTER 8:
Wrapping Up

"The future ain't what it use to be."

– Yogi Berra

I grew up playing baseball as a kid, so I thought it a fitting occasion to end the book with a relevant quote from a legend of the game.

For the past year every source I have read and expert panels I have listened to all make mention about living in a customer-led business world where business innovation is the new way to successfully compete. Consumers are now demanding qualitative outcomes from companies – something missing from past decades.

It's no longer about simply having the best brand. Consumer materialism, once the heartbeat of western economies, has given way to social media. Buyers are now armed to very publically provide reviews, ratings and likes/dislikes for a product or service. The amount of time for news to travel has shortened from days to hours, even minutes.

These new social platforms have also created a greater awareness to societal responsibility. Many now ask what societal value is being generated, or perhaps being harmed by a business before they perform a transaction. For businesses it's now profit with purpose as opposed to profit before purpose. Greed is out and community mindfulness in.

What does this mean for management teams? Unlike the past three decades, no longer do operational efficiencies guarantee a business's success. Customers are now challenging a business's role in the customer value chain. It doesn't matter if the business is a supplier, distributor or wholesaler. Customers want to know where goods are sourced from and who makes them. User experiences and customer loyalty programs are the new business priorities of the day, replacing the priority for releasing new product enhancements and features.

For a business to be effective, its leadership must seek a return to the basics to rediscover what I call, the human condition. To think not just about the customer but also about the employees who work for it.

As our world increasingly becomes technologically interconnected, there is a greater self-awareness of who we are, what we desire to be and how we can affect change. Business practices that better align to these humanistic conditions are reaping those wealth benefits. The widening use of technology offers an accelerated channel to turn business success into a reality. The introduction of many new cross-functional C-Level roles attests to how technology's impact continues to climb up the corporate ladder.

Management must think about transforming their business from the inside out to become more innovatively competitive. What existing internal mechanisms, if any, are suited for this transformation journey? In most organisations making a journey of this significance is something quite different from the past way of operating.

The art of strategic management is well positioned to assist in making the journey successful. I'm not arguing for a need to radically rethink strategy. The theory behind competition has not changed and the science of strategy still remains one-part thinking and one-part execution. What has changed is the mechanics of performing good execution.

In a past world where operational efficiencies were king, business silos reigned supreme. There was no need to coordinate strategic execution. Each silo went about this independently. Yet today one poor performing business unit could now set back the entirely organisation.

To effectively compete, management needs to depart from silo business thinking. Command and control management environments, which reinforce silo decision-making practices, remain one of the most daunting challenges for an organisation today.

These environments are slower to act and also breed specialist roles, keeping them locked in. Yet to deliver a holistic customer approach requires quicker response time and broad, instead of specialised, knowledge. This broad knowledge is imperative in anchoring a formidable strategic execution plan, or roadmap.

It all means that the application of strategic management today requires a different approach and set of skills from yesteryear. A strategic plan today requires a multi-disciplinary approach that tightly weaves in human capital practices and technology innovation to traditional anchors of finance and marketing.

The megatrend where consumers with their technology devices demand immediate attention requires full recognition by the executive management team and board. Integration of organisational change management and the technology channel must be critical part of any transformation initiative. The broad-based strategist is absolutely critical in their role to navigate the particularities of each discipline. They cast an objective eye to each, without any specialised prejudices.

Performing strategic management assumes one critical component – strong and unwavering leadership. All organisations start and stop with their leadership.

If leadership is perceived weak, in conflict or simply ineffective, it will significantly dilute the effectiveness of the strategic management practices. These practices will become a burden on the organisation, draining capital, causing un-necessary work stress and potentially damaging the reputation of the organisation. If poor leadership exists, do not perform strategic planning until leadership issues are addressed. The risks are just too high.

There's a convergence underway bringing technology innovation, greater societal self-awareness and increasing reliance of instant information anywhere, all closer together. It is a world forcing organisations to not only adapt to a new set of operating rules, but also consider their social impact to the communities and people affected by their presence. Those organisations that make the leap first, stand to gain greater wealth and prosperity.

The value of executing business strategy needs to be immediately rethought, rewritten and reprogrammed for this new context. The new way of doing things is only hampered by the old ways of doing things.

I strongly believe businesses should return to age-old concepts of common sense, authenticity and sound wisdom. These people-infused principles have been neglected in the strategic corridors for far too long.

Organisations need people who can champion these principles. People who possess deep experiences, combined with the ability to laterally think, and who can communicate to broad diverse audiences. People equipped to connect multi-disciplinary dots to better position the organisation for future growth.

The once meandering river of business competition, based largely on quantifying operational efficiency gains, is no longer. It's time to begin designing and building a new boat capable of withstanding the repetitive waves of consumer disruption. A people-focused strategist who understands these conditions and expected length of that journey can navigate safe passage to the river delta and a blue ocean of opportunities.

BIBLIOGRAPHY

ANZ Bank. "The Breakout Story: transforming the culture of ANZ." *ANZ Bank.* Assessed 5 September 2014. http://www.anz.com.au/australia/support/library/mr/breakoutstory020207.pdf

Bersin, Josh. 13 March 2015. "Culture: Why It's The Hottest Topic In Business Today." *Forbes.* Assessed 3 April 2015. http://www.forbes.com/sites/joshbersin/2015/03/13/culture-why-its-the-hottest-topic-in-business-today/

Birshan, Michael, Renee Dye and Stephen Hall. January 2011. "Creating more value with corporate strategy: McKinsey Global Survey results." *McKinsey & Company.* Accessed 28 May 2014. http://www.mckinsey.com/insights/strategy/creating_more_value_with_corporate_strategy_mckinsey_global_survey_results

Branson, Richard. 2013. *Screw Business as Usual.* Random House Group.

Busch, Jason. 21 February 2013. "The AP Invoicing Exception Epidemic: Is it really THIS bad? (Part 1)." *Spend Matters Network.* Assessed 25 June 2015. https://spendmatters.com/2013/02/21/the-ap-invoicing-exception-epidemic-is-it-really-this-bad-part-1/

Cherry, Christophe. "What a Mexican cement company can teach you about innovation." *Whiteboard.* Assessed 16 June 2014. http://www.whiteboardmag.com/what-a-mexican-cement-company-can-teach-you-about-innovation/

Cohen, Yaacov. 30 June 2011. "Coping With Distractions: 6 ways You Can Boost Your Productivity." *Forbes*. Accessed 30 July 2014. http://www.forbes.com/sites/ciocentral/2011/06/30/coping-with-distractions-6-ways-you-can-boost-your-productivity/

Crabbe, Tony. 2014. Busy: How to thrive in a world of too much. Piatkus Books.

Ditmore, Jim. 28 October 2013. "Why Do Big IT Projects Fail So Often?" *Information Week*. Accessed 28 July 2014. http://www.informationweek.com/strategic-cio/executive-insights-and-innovation/why-do-big-it-projects-fail-so-often/d/d-id/1112087

Emmons, Garry. 1 March 2010. Review of *Lords of Strategy,* by Walter Kiechel. *Harvard Business School*. Accessed 01 June 2014. https://www.alumni.hbs.edu/stories/Pages/story-bulletin.aspx?num=88

Freeman, Ed. "Stakeholder Theory." Keynote Speech, Liberating The Heroic Spirit of Business from Conscious Capitalism Australia, Sydney, Australia, 24 June 2014.

Gavett, Gretchen. 9 July 2014. "What you need to know about segmentation." *Harvard Business Review*. Accessed 21 July 2014. http://blogs.hbr.org/2014/07/what-you-need-to-know-about-segmentation/

Gibson, Rowan. 26 January 2013. "Efficiency versus Value – The New Innovation Equation." *Innovation Excellence*. Accessed 19 April 2014. http://www.innovationexcellence.com/blog/2013/01/26/up-or-down-innovation-and-value-are-key/

GilPress. 4 February 2013. "The Big Data Explosion (Infographic)." *A CoupMedia Infographic*. Accessed 8 July 2014. http://whatsthebigdata.com/2013/02/04/the-big-data-explosion-infographic/

Gino, Francesca, Lisa D Ordonez, and David Welsh. 4 September 2014. "How Unethical Behavior Becomes Habit." *Harvard Business Review Blog Network*. Assessed 9 September 2014. http://blogs.hbr.org/2014/09/how-unethical-behavior-becomes-habit/

BIBLIOGRAPHY

Greber, Jacob. 11 June 2014. "Reserve Bank's Sarv Girn says companies must innovate or die." *The Australian Financial Review.* Accessed 13 June 2014. http://m.afr.com/p/technology/reserve_bank_sarv_girn_says_compani es_hR0kMkXEuEk7owwFNZxdgP

Hall, Ashley 23 March 2011. "Japan disaster's 'ripple effect' on Australian auto industry." *ABC News.* Accessed 7 June 2014. http://www.abc.net.au/news/2011-03-23/japan-disasters-ripple-effect-on-australian-auto/2646216

Kaston, Carren O., Susan Porter Benson, Robert Ferrell, James Flink, Ellis Hawley, Susan Smulyan, and Joe William Trotter. 14 August 1995. "Taylorism and Economic Efficiency in the 1920s; The Coolidge Era and the Consumer Economy, 1921-1929." *Library of Congress.* Accessed 14 August 2014. http://lcweb2.loc.gov:8081/ammem/amrlhtml/intaylor.html

Kiechel, Walter. 28 October 2010. "Strategy as a Case to Be Cracked." *Chief Executive Officer.* Accessed 11 August 2014. http://www.the-chiefexecutive.com/features/feature99871/

Kleiner, Art. 2003. "GE's Next Workout." *Strategy + Business.* Issue 33. Accessed 19 April 2014. http://www.strategy-business.com/article/03403?

Lazauskas, Joe. 6 August 2014. "How to Avoid a CMO vs. CIO War." *Forbes BrandVoice.* Assessed 11 August 2014. http://www.forbes.com/sites/centurylink/2014/08/06/how-to-avoid-a-cmo-vs-cio-war/

Livingstone, Rob. 24 May 2014. "What's your IT department's role in preventing a data breach?" *RLA: Rob Livingstone Advisory.* Accessed 7 June 2014. http://rob-livingstone.com/2014/05/whats-departments-role-preventing-data-breach/

Lund, Dr Paddi. 1997. *Building The Happiness-Centred Business.* Solutions Press.

Martin, Roger. 12 June 2014. "Why smart people struggle with strategy." *Harvard Business Review Blog Network.* Accessed 17 June

2014. http://blogs.hbr.org/2014/06/why-smart-people-struggle-with-strategy/

Metwally, Ahmed, Divyakant Agrawal and Amr El Abbadi. June 2006. "Hide and Seek: Detecting Hit Inflation Fraud in Streams of Web Advertising Networks." *Department of Computer Science, University of California at Santa Barbara.*

Owl, Orchid. 20 September 2007. "Kaizen." *Business Management Consulting Theories and Models.* Accessed 4 May 2014. http://business-management-consulting.blogspot.com.au/2007/09/kaizen.html

Plant, Robert. 16 July 2014. "IT Has Finally Cracked the C-Suite." *Harvard Business Review Blog Network.* Assessed 19 August 2014. http://blogs.hbr.org/2014/07/it-has-finally-cracked-the-c-suite/

Porter, Michael E, W. Chan Kim, and Renee Mauborgne. 2011. *On Strategy.* Harvard Business Review Press.

Pro Bono Australia. 2014. "Community Development." *Pro Bono Australia.* Accessed 15 September 2014. http://www.probonoaustralia.com.au/corporate-community/community-development

Prosci. 2015. "What is Change Management." *Prosci, Inc.* http://www.prosci.com/change-management/definition/

Pursuit of Happiness, Inc. "Abraham Maslow." *The pursuit of happiness.* Accessed 5 May 2014. http://www.pursuit-of-happiness.org/history-of-happiness/abraham-maslow/

SingTel Optus. 2014. "Creating a Business Your Customers Love: Optus Future of Business Report 2014." *SingTel Optus Pty Ltd.* Assessed 6 July 2014. http://yesopt.us/fob14

Skibola, Nicole. 12 November 2010. "CEMEX Blazes the Social Innovation Trail." *Forbes Online.* Assessed 16 June 2014. http://www.forbes.com/sites/csr/2010/11/12/blazing-the-social-innovation-trail-cemex-continues-to-thrive/

The Energy Project. 2015. *The Energy Project*. Assessed 25 May 2015. http://theenergyproject.com/key-ideas

Timson, Lia. 30 July 2014. "Australia nears digital tipping point, Deloitte Media Consumer Survey shows." *Sydney Morning Herald*. Accessed 30 July 2014. http://www.smh.com.au/digital-life/digital-life-news/australia-nears-digital-tipping-point-deloitte-media-consumer-survey-shows-20140730-zygr9.html

Traveler. 9 March 2009. "Debunked: "kaizen = Japanese philosophy of continuous improvement." *Home Japan*. Accessed 17 September 2014. http://www.homejapan.com/2009/03/debunked-kaizen

Winerman, Lea. March 2013. "Smarter than Ever?" *Monitor on Psychology*. Vol 44, No3. Assessed 22 August 2014. http://www.apa.org/monitor/2013/03/smarter.aspx

Woods, Dan. 14 April 2014. "Don't let a Chief Digital Officer steal the best part of your job." *Forbes*. Accessed 15 June 2014. http://www.forbes.com/sites/danwoods/2014/04/14/dont-let-a-chief-digital-officer-steal-the-best-part-of-your-job/

Wooldridge, Adrian. 12 March 2010. "Big Think In the Boardroom: How business moved from affable amateurism to specialized, intellectualized 'models' and expertise." *Wall Street Journal*.
http://online.wsj.com/news/articles/SB10001424052748704869304575109591109900792?tesla=y